WINDSOR CASTLE

WINDSOR CASTLE

Pamela Hartshorne

ROYAL COLLECTION TRUST

CONTENTS

INTRODUCTION

Founded by William the Conqueror in the 1070s, Windsor Castle is one of the oldest castles in the world. It is also one of the largest. Its curtain wall encloses the State Apartments and The Queen's private apartments; the College of St George and St George's Chapel, spiritual home of the Order of the Garter; the Royal Library and Archives; an outstanding collection of art and furniture; a military garrison and a working kitchen that dates back to the fourteenth century.

Continuously occupied since the eleventh century, the castle has been rebuilt, renovated, remodelled and redecorated over the centuries according to the needs, interests and ambitions of successive monarchs. Today it is a busy working palace, its richly decorated interior contrasting with the austere façade that harks back to its fortress origins.

Throughout its long history Windsor Castle has served as an impressive backdrop for the ceremonial of diplomacy and kingship, but it has also been an intimate place. It is home to Her Majesty The Queen and the setting for many of the Royal Family's private gatherings, as it has been for previous generations. For more than nine centuries kings and queens, their children and courtiers, as well as soldiers and servants, gardeners and cleaners, chaplains, conservators and cooks and countless others have lived and worked at the castle.

This is their story. It is an account less of the art and architecture of Windsor Castle – remarkable though they are – than of the events that have shaped it over the past thousand years and of the people who have transformed it from a simple wooden fortification on the banks of the River Thames to one of the most spectacular castles in the world.

Giltwood overmantel mirror designed by Morel & Seddon for the Grand Reception Room

With their lavish use of gilt and elaborate ornamentation, Morel & Seddon's interior designs for George IV (1762–1830) transformed the castle and created a striking contrast between the austere exterior and the sumptuously decorated rooms.

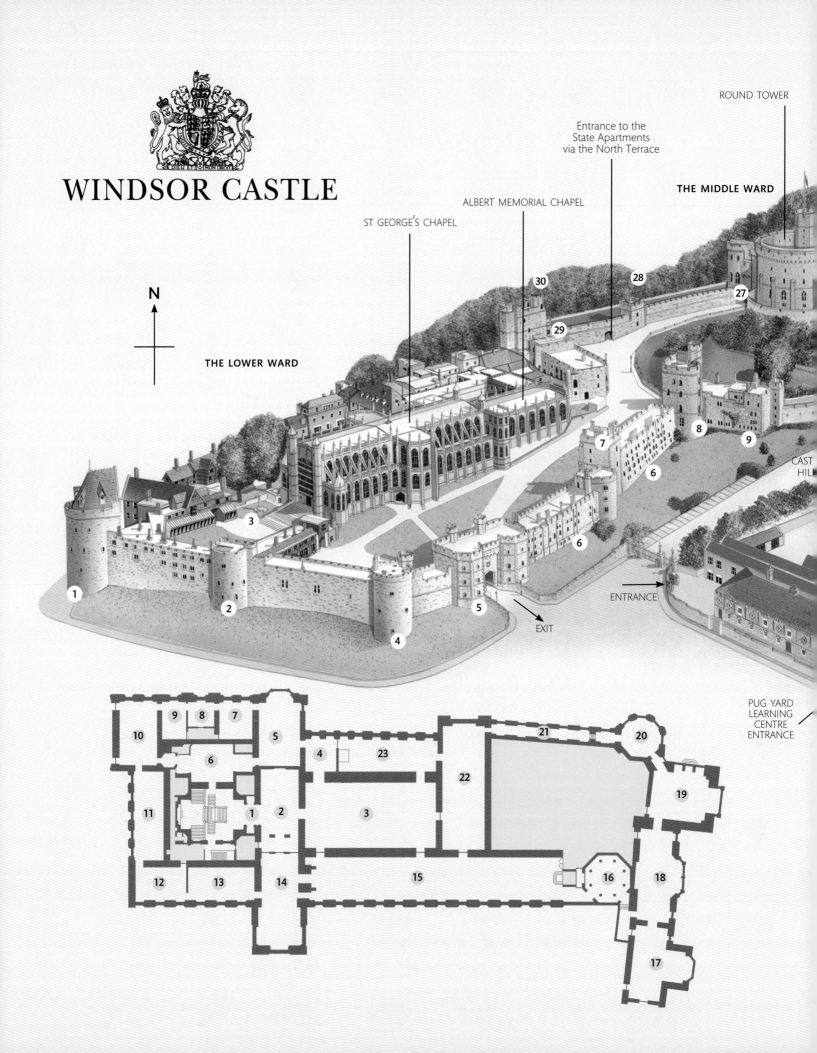

WINDSOR CASTLE

ROUND TOWER

Entrance to the
State Apartments
via the North Terrace

ALBERT MEMORIAL CHAPEL

THE MIDDLE WARD

ST GEORGE'S CHAPEL

N

THE LOWER WARD

CAST
HIL

ENTRANCE

EXIT

PUG YARD
LEARNING
CENTRE
ENTRANCE

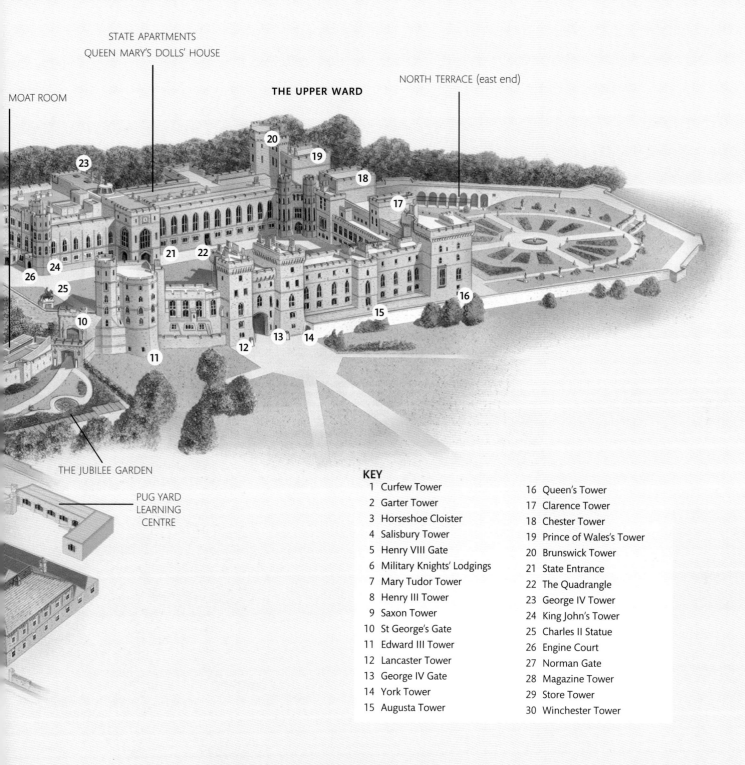

MOAT ROOM

STATE APARTMENTS
QUEEN MARY'S DOLLS' HOUSE

THE UPPER WARD

NORTH TERRACE (east end)

THE JUBILEE GARDEN

PUG YARD
LEARNING
CENTRE

KEY

1	Curfew Tower	16	Queen's Tower
2	Garter Tower	17	Clarence Tower
3	Horseshoe Cloister	18	Chester Tower
4	Salisbury Tower	19	Prince of Wales's Tower
5	Henry VIII Gate	20	Brunswick Tower
6	Military Knights' Lodgings	21	State Entrance
7	Mary Tudor Tower	22	The Quadrangle
8	Henry III Tower	23	George IV Tower
9	Saxon Tower	24	King John's Tower
10	St George's Gate	25	Charles II Statue
11	Edward III Tower	26	Engine Court
12	Lancaster Tower	27	Norman Gate
13	George IV Gate	28	Magazine Tower
14	York Tower	29	Store Tower
15	Augusta Tower	30	Winchester Tower

THE STATE APARTMENTS

KEY

1	Grand Staircase	9	King's Closet	17	Green Drawing Room
2	Grand Vestibule	10	Queen's Drawing Room	18	Crimson Drawing Room
3	Waterloo Chamber	11	Queen's Gallery	19	State Dining Room
4	Ante-Throne Room	12	Queen's Audience Chamber	20	Octagon Dining Room
5	King's Drawing Room	13	Queen's Presence Chamber	21	China Corridor
6	King's Dining Room	14	Queen's Guard Chamber	22	Grand Reception Room
7	King's Bedchamber	15	St George's Hall	23	Garter Throne Room
8	King's Dressing Room	16	Lantern Lobby		

1

THE MEDIEVAL CASTLE

For many, Windsor Castle embodies an idea of England, of strength, of stability and of a proud heritage, its distinctive silhouette a symbol of the British monarchy itself. It is easy to forget that it was founded by conquering invaders from what is now France. The decisive victory of William, Duke of Normandy, over the last Saxon king, Harold I, at the Battle of Hastings in 1066 left him in possession of the throne, and he was crowned King William I of England in Westminster Abbey on Christmas Day

that same year. In retrospect the Norman Conquest of England seems inevitable, but at the time William's hold on the Crown was far from secure, and he faced resistance from the defeated Anglo-Saxons for many years.

The castle at Windsor was one of many that were constructed across the country as part of an often brutal campaign to subjugate the English rebels. For the Normans, castles were not only military and administrative centres but also highly symbolic buildings, which dominated the countryside in a way

Left: Situated on a bluff overlooking the river, Windsor Castle was built to defend one of the key routes into London along the Thames Valley.

Right: Earl Harold (centre) swearing an oath of allegiance to William, Duke of Normandy: a scene from the Bayeux Tapestry, 1070s. Harold's breaking of the oath prompted William's invasion of England.

A conjectural reconstruction of the original motte and bailey castle at Windsor, around 1086. The motte, one of the largest ever built in England, still stands at the heart of the castle.

that had not been seen in England before. The 'fortifications that the Normans called castles were scarcely known in the English provinces', explained the historian Orderic Vitalis, 'and so the English in spite of their courage and love of fighting could put up only a weak resistance to their enemies.'

When the Norman castle builders arrived at Windsor at some point in the 1070s, they found an ideal site. A day's march from London, there was an established settlement nearby at what is now known as Old Windsor, where the Saxon kings had built a royal hall, close to both the River Thames and the great forest where they hunted. The hall at

Old Windsor continued to be used by the Norman kings, but the new castle was situated at New Windsor, on a ridge to the north west overlooking the Thames upstream, where there may well already have been a crossing-point. The site gave distant views and an easily defensible position while providing access to the river and protecting a key route into London along the Thames Valley.

The first castle at Windsor was constructed to a typical Norman motte and bailey design: a man-made earthen mound known as a motte was surrounded by a bailey or enclosed area, protected in its turn by a wooden fence and a broad ditch. A simple wooden keep, or fortified tower, stood on top of the mound. The motte at Windsor was one of the largest ever built in England and still survives, today topped by the twelfth-century Round Tower. The first bailey became known as the Middle Ward, but was later eclipsed by the much larger Lower and Upper Wards.

Initially the castle was occupied by a military garrison, charged with enforcing the king's authority. The Saxon royal hall at Old Windsor remained one of the pre-eminent royal residences, and the Norman kings continued to hold court there until the early twelfth century. The excellent hunting in the forest nearby was a draw, as it remained for successive monarchs until the nineteenth century.

It was Henry I who first established Windsor Castle as a residence in about 1110, constructing a group of stone buildings known as the King's Houses in what is now called the Upper Ward. Recently discovered archaeological evidence suggests that these buildings were imposing one- or two-storey structures, richly ornamented in the Romanesque style. They included

a hall, chamber and chapel as well as the usual service buildings. The King's Houses provided the setting for the first recorded royal wedding held at the castle when the widowed Henry, then 53, married Adeliza, daughter of the Count of Louvain and Brussels and some 35 years younger than the king, on 24 January 1121. Adeliza was consecrated Queen with much ceremony at the castle shortly afterwards. A Great Hall with adjacent buildings was erected in the Lower Ward about this time, too, probably during Henry I's reign.

The King's Houses were witness to one of the pivotal events of the twelfth century. The death of Henry's only son and heir in the wreck of the *White Ship* in 1120 meant that his daughter, Matilda, became his sole legitimate heir. Anxious to secure her succession, Henry summoned the lords of the realm to the Christmas court at Windsor in 1126 and commanded them to make oaths of allegiance to his daughter, swearing to uphold her rights of succession in both England and Normandy. After Henry's death in 1135, England was riven by a bitter civil war between the nobles who believed that the oath they had sworn at Windsor was binding, and those convinced that Matilda's cousin,

Romanesque stonework from the twelfth-century King's Houses at Windsor

Surviving fragments of carving suggest that the first royal residence at Windsor built by Henry I (*c*.1068–1135) was an impressive group of stone buildings.

Above: A reconstruction of the castle as it may have appeared during the 1216 siege shows the development of the three distinct Wards – Upper, Middle and Lower – that have survived to this day.

Opposite: The sallyport in the Curfew Tower. This underground passage was built to allow defenders to leave the castle undetected in times of siege. It has survived virtually unchanged since the thirteenth century.

Stephen (son of the Conqueror's daughter Adela), would be a more effective leader than a woman. The savagery of the conflict caused untold suffering across the country; according to the *Peterborough Chronicle*, 'men said openly that Christ and his saints slept'. The conflict was ended only when Stephen acknowledged Matilda's son, Henry Plantagenet, as his heir.

Henry II, as he became in 1154, was a charismatic character and his queen, Eleanor of Aquitaine, an equally forceful personality. They had eight children, including four quarrelsome sons, Henry, Richard, Geoffrey

and John. It was from Windsor that King John rode out to Runnymede Meadow (beyond Old Windsor, to the south west) in 1215 and swore to uphold Magna Carta, the charter of liberties drawn up by his barons in the hope of curbing royal power. John's treacherous attempts to seize the throne from his brother, Richard I, had alienated many, and his increasingly tyrannical behaviour once king

men said openly that Christ and his saints slept

lost him further support. In one notorious case, he captured the wife and eldest son of William de Briouze and incarcerated them at Windsor Castle, where they starved to death. Driven to outright rebellion, the disaffected barons offered the throne to Louis, son of Philip II of France, who brought an army to England in May 1216, and besieged Windsor Castle that summer. The siege lasted more than two months, during which time the southern side of the motte collapsed, probably as the result of a mining operation by the besiegers.

John's death in Newark on 18 October 1216 brought an end to the conflict but the siege had revealed how vulnerable Windsor Castle was to attack, and a number of works carried out during the minority of John's son, Henry III, were designed to repair the damage and to improve defences. A circuit of curtain walls was completed, increasing the enclosed area to 13 acres (5.2 hectares). Restored over the centuries, the walls have defined the boundaries of Windsor Castle ever since. The motte was shored up and in 1225 the present Round Tower replaced an earlier stone keep. The construction of a pair of underground sallyports leading to the castle ditch may also date from this time. These could be used in the event of a further siege and allow the defenders to make surprise attacks. The castle was also equipped with the latest in military technology, a trebuchet, a type of huge catapult with a long arm and massive counterweight that enabled it to fling heavy stones over the castle wall; this was one of the first trebuchets to be seen in England.

But the greatest changes to the castle came during the later years of Henry III's reign, which ushered in a new and richer era in the history of English royal building and court culture. Like previous kings, Henry III spent much of the year at Westminster, but

from the late 1230s onwards Windsor Castle was established as the monarch's principal residence outside London. For the first time, too, the castle was used as a family home. In 1236 Henry, then aged 28, married Eleanor, the 12-year-old daughter of the Count of Provence, and their first child, Edward, was born in 1239, followed by Margaret, Beatrice (called 'Beautiful B' by her father) and Edmund. A fifth child, Katherine, was born in 1253. Described as beautiful but 'dumb and helpless', the little princess died, probably at Windsor, when she was four.

After Margaret's birth in 1240, Henry decided to transform the King's Houses in the Upper Ward into a more spacious and secluded residence for his family. Three new towers were built along the north curtain wall and two new chambers provided for the royal children who grew up in the castle. Eight sons of noble families lived at Windsor with them, and another eight boys or young men from gentry families acted as valets or esquires.

The children's household numbered at least 30. In 1254 it included four unnamed ladies, Richard, the chaplain, a cleric called Simon de Wycombe, six yeomen, Master Godwin, the cook, and a laundress, and was part of a larger resident community at Windsor. During Henry III's reign the number of those living at the castle grew to well over a hundred: knights, serjeants, upper servants and craftsmen, all of whom had their own families and servants, and doubtless many more servants and labourers, all under the command of the Constable, who was in charge of the castle on behalf of the sovereign. There were separate kitchens in the Upper Ward to serve the royal children and the queen when she was in residence, but the bulk of the castle's inhabitants ate in the Great Hall, which was served by kitchens in the Lower Ward.

Painted head by Master William of Westminster, *c*.1248

Henry III's 'Great Chapel' was lavishly furnished and decorated with vividly painted figures like this small head now reset within the narthex to the Albert Memorial Chapel.

Henry III was famous for his piety and tried to live up to the idea of the king as protector of those in need. The castle's almoner made regular distributions of leftover food from the Almonry in the Lower Ward, and wherever the king was staying he ordered large numbers of poor people to be fed every day. On major religious festivals hundreds at a time were also fed in all his main residences. On Christmas Eve 1239, 15 Windsor paupers received food and were given shoes costing a penny each 'for the good state and health of Edward the King's son'. The following year the Great Hall and a smaller hall in the castle were filled with the destitute who were given a meal on Easter Day, and on the Friday of

On Christmas Eve 1239, 15 Windsor paupers were fed and given shoes costing a penny each 'for the good state and health of Edward the King's son'

Whitsun week when Henry ordered that 'as many poor as will fill the great hall and the hall in the upper bailey' were to be fed.

Generous as Henry was to the least fortunate in society, the money he spent on charity paled into insignificance compared

to the £15,000 he lavished on Windsor Castle during his reign. The Lower Ward was transformed by the building of a magnificent new chapel where the Albert Memorial Chapel now stands. Dedicated to St Edward the Confessor and the Virgin Mary, the chapel was 70 ft (23.3 m) in length and 28 ft (8.5 m) in breadth and had a high wooden roof painted to look as if it were made of stone. Henry took a personal interest in the design and specified good wainscoting and painting, a lead roof and a stone turret to house three or four bells. Served by four chaplains, the new chapel was supplied with books, plate and vestments, together with a 'great and beautiful basin', which was probably for washing hands before Mass. Only a few fragments of works of art from this period made for the chapel survive; those that do, including some paintings of heads and the original chapel door with its beautiful scrolling ironwork (the 'Gilebertus' door), suggest that the chapel must have been splendid indeed when it was complete.

The works that Henry ordered for both the Upper and the Lower Wards must have had a similarly dramatic effect. The King's Houses grew into a sprawling complex occupying most of the area of the present State Apartments. The main chambers probably consisted of two floors, with service rooms for wardrobes or servants' accommodation below and royal chambers above. Many of the rooms appear to have had panelling with painted walls above. The panelling was also often painted: a new chamber adjoining the queen's chamber was green with gold stars, while another favourite scheme was to paint the wainscot green with a pattern of sun rays. The windows in the king's chamber were glazed, a rarity at the time, but in most other rooms the draughts were kept out by timber shutters, as brightly decorated as everything else. Sometimes the walls were painted to resemble textile hangings or even ashlar masonry, while some may have had more elaborate schemes, such as that incorporating roundels with signs of the Zodiac which survives in fragmentary form in a thirteenth-century chamber of a house in the Cloisters of the Lower Ward.

Henry's changes turned the Upper Ward into a separate residence to which most visitors to the castle were unlikely to have had access, and to which he could retire with his family and inner chamber staff. The more public business of government still took place in the Great Hall and the royal apartments in the Lower Ward, where the queen had her own chamber so that she could participate in state occasions.

Henry III left Windsor for the last time in June 1272 and died in November that year. Although one of the greatest of royal builders, his passion for architecture and decoration was not matched by political acumen and his reign was marked by rebellion and intrigue. His son and heir,

Edward I, was a much more capable strategist but spent most of his own reign on campaign and was rarely at Windsor, although it continued as a royal nursery for several years under the supervision of the widowed Queen Eleanor. In 1295 Henry III's new chambers in the Lower Ward were destroyed by fire and abandoned.

On Edward I's death in 1307 he was succeeded by his son, Edward II, who had little interest in the castle, preferring to stay at a manor house in the Great Park to the south when at Windsor. His grandfather's splendid palace slowly decayed and was used instead as a comfortable prison, lodging a number of Scottish prisoners of war, most notably in 1312 Elizabeth, wife of Robert II Bruce of Scotland. By the time of Edward III's accession in 1327 Windsor Castle was in a sorry state, the Lower Ward marred by the blackened ruins of Henry III's royal lodgings

Warrior king and founder of the Order of the Garter, Edward III transformed Windsor Castle into a centre of a Christian, chivalric monarchy. His portrait, which hangs in St George's Chapel, was commissioned in 1615.

the castle was recast as Camelot, a centre of chivalry, honour and prestige

while the palatial apartments in the Upper Ward were rarely used. Under Edward, however, Windsor Castle underwent an extraordinary renaissance. The remains of Henry III's impressive palace were swept away and the castle recast as Camelot, a centre of chivalry, honour and prestige.

An astute king and an outstanding military commander, Edward III had learnt from his father's humiliating defeat by the Scots at Bannockburn in 1314. If he was to pursue his ambition to reclaim his ancestral lands in France, he would need a new and better-trained knightly class. The regular jousts and tournaments he organised were intended not only to train knights in the use of arms but also to promote an *esprit de corps*. During the 1330s these events took place almost monthly in the summer and on major feast days in winter. They could be highly theatrical, the participants sometimes in exotic disguises, but the tournaments were by no means just for show and on occasion could end in serious injury or even death.

In addition to improving the performance of his knights, Edward III set about restoring the image of the monarchy, which had suffered badly under his father. He had a flair for what would today be called 'public relations' and cultivated a myth connecting his reign with that of King Arthur. Associating himself with the legendary king, Edward brought together a company of highly motivated and trained knights deliberately recalling those of Arthur's Round Table. In January 1344 a great festival was held at

Windsor Castle: the Great Kitchen, after restoration, by Alexander Creswell, 1999 Built by Edward III, the Great Kitchen is still in use today.

Windsor Castle at which Edward announced the founding of a new chivalric order of the Round Table that would embrace all the nobility and senior knights and create a new Camelot to emulate the ideals of Arthurian chivalry. The festival involved feasting, dancing and various entertainments, as well as three days of jousting and an oath of allegiance to the new order. Afterwards, Edward ordered 'that a most noble building be built, in which to hold the Round Table, and instructed masons, carpenters and other workmen to carry out the work'.

Excavations in 2006 found evidence of this extraordinary structure in the Upper Ward. It was a vast circular building which seems to have been intended to house the Round Table, but Edward's enthusiasm for the project evidently cooled, perhaps because of lack of money, and the 'noble building' was dismantled before it was finished. However, his victory over the French army at Crécy in 1346 prompted him to found the very much more enduring Order of the Garter (see pp. 30–3).

Edward's plans for the new Order involved major rebuilding in both the Lower and Upper Wards and for many years the castle was the largest building site in England.

The initial work was planned and overseen by William of Wykeham, later Bishop of Winchester and Chancellor of England. William was said to have been 'of very low birth' but 'very shrewd and a man of great industry'. The pace of building was slow at first, largely due to the chronic shortage of labour that followed the Black Death. A particularly virulent strain of the bubonic plague, the Black Death raged across the country between June 1348 and December 1349 and may have carried off a third of England's population. Sheriffs across the country were commanded to send masons, stonecutters, stonelayers and other labourers to work at Windsor Castle, on pain of heavy fines if they failed, 'for the business is near the King's heart'. Other workmen were pressed into service in the same way: glaziers, plasterers, painters, smiths, plumbers, tilers, carters, limeburners and general labourers. In the early 1360s the total workforce present at any one time must have exceeded a thousand, all of whom had to be housed, fed and organised.

for the business is near the King's heart

Opposite: The Norman Gate and Moat Garden

Although remodelled in the nineteenth century, the misleadingly named Norman Gate was in fact built by Edward III to control access to the Upper Ward. Today the Governor of the Castle lives in the Norman Gate, while the moat surrounding the Round Tower is maintained as a garden attached to the residence.

The work did not stop the court gathering regularly at Windsor for the Christmas or Easter feasts, and, of course, for the annual Garter Feast. Until the new royal lodgings were completed in 1365, the king and Queen Philippa stayed in temporary chambers in the Round Tower. At its peak in 1360, their joint household numbered about 580. They, too, had to be fed and accommodated at the castle, which must often have been bulging at the seams.

October 1361 saw another royal wedding celebrated at the castle, when Edward III's heir, the Black Prince, married Joan of Kent. In spite of the fact that only half the castle was available for use, it must have been a splendid gathering, attended by Edward III's sister, Joan, Queen of Scotland, and many members of the English nobility. Edward's daughter, Isabella, was also married at Windsor, to the French nobleman Enguerrand de Coucy, in a lavish ceremony in July 1365, an occasion for which the king spent £4,500 on jewels and plate alone.

By 1365 the royal lodgings in the Upper Ward were finished, completing the transformation of the castle. In the Lower Ward, Henry's chapel remained, but had been rededicated to St George, as well as to the Virgin Mary and St Edward. Its role and scale of operations were transformed by the establishment in 1348 of the College of St George as the spiritual arm of the Order of the Garter, and the initial building work provided accommodation for the canons and vicars to come together every day to pray and celebrate Mass in the Great Chapel. Lodgings were also provided for the Poor Knights, appointed to attend Mass on behalf of the Knight Companions who were often busy elsewhere.

There is no evidence for paving in the Lower Ward, and the surface of beaten clay and chalk must have become either very muddy or very dusty on occasion. It was doubtless a busy place, with servants, choristers, grooms, soldiers and workmen criss-crossing the Ward. The main gate to the castle was manned by a 'janitor' and the Almonry, where the poor still queued to receive food as they had done in the time of Henry III, probably stood to one side of the gate, against the wall.

At the head of the Lower Ward stood the twelfth-century wall with a simple gatehouse. This was the chief checkpoint to the Middle

Ward and Upper Ward beyond until 1359–61, when a new gateway to the Upper Ward, now known as the Norman Gate, was built. The building has been well preserved, and today includes part of the Governor of the Castle's residence. His desk in one of the upper rooms sits against what might have been the upper part of the original portcullis.

A visitor passing through the new gateway in the later fourteenth century could not have failed to have been impressed by the majestic dimensions of the courtyard beyond. By then the Quadrangle (as it is known today) was probably turfed and crossed with informal beaten earth paths. The sheer size of the Quadrangle suggests that it may well have been used as a setting for tournaments and other military displays, although there is no conclusive proof of this.

Two-storey buildings on the east and south side of the Quadrangle provided spacious lodgings for high-ranking courtiers and other important visitors, while the heart of the palace was the huge range on the north side of the Ward that housed the royal apartments. This austerely impressive building incorporated masonry from the twelfth and thirteenth centuries, and although it has been extensively rebuilt since, the shell survives within the present State Apartments, the essential outlines of which remain as set out in Edward III's time.

The royal lodgings were arranged around three inner courtyards. A Great Gate signalled the main entrance, which led eventually into a central courtyard with a doorway to the Great Stair. At the top of the steps, doorways from a broad landing led to the principal areas of the royal residence. To the left were the queen's apartments, to the right, the king's, while the third doorway led straight into the Great Hall. This magnificent room, some 123 ft (37.5 m) long, lit by

115 mirrors fixed to the ceiling

11 windows on the south wall, would eventually be extended to become St George's Hall as we see it today. Tapestries or painted hangings could be displayed on the windowless north wall, while at the far (east) end the king's table sat on a dais. In the fourteenth century the floor was probably paved in stone and there may have been two fires in central hearths, the smoke vented by louvres in the high timber roof.

The Great Hall was used for state occasions such as Garter feasts, but the king and queen normally dined elsewhere. On a day-to-day level the Hall was home to the lower household servants. Meals were served there in two sittings, and many servants probably also slept in the Hall.

The king's apartments were reached through a Guard Room that led into the king's Great Chamber. Although not as long as the Great Hall, it was a large, light room with tall windows overlooking the Quadrangle, and was used for public audiences and courtly entertainments. The king also had a bathhouse on the ground floor, equipped with two 'great vats' and glazed windows. Above was his First Chamber. This may have been where Edward actually slept, or perhaps a study, with a private chapel opening off it. The Rose Tower at the south-west corner of his apartments contained an octagonal room, its vaulted ceiling decorated with bosses in the shape of roses, and stairs led up to a 'Painted Chamber' above. Both were small rooms that were probably used for intimate gatherings.

Queen Philippa had separate north-facing apartments, with her own Great Chamber, and beyond that a 'chamber with mirrors', which had 115 mirrors fixed to the ceiling. Mirrors were luxury items at the time and they must have made a dazzling display. Otherwise, the royal apartments were light and spacious, but sparingly decorated. Most of the rooms seem to have been painted with a yellow-gold ochre wash, while the floors tended to be paved with glazed tiles. The furniture, too, was plain and generally portable, reflecting the itinerant nature of court life. The royal chambers could be quickly transformed with tapestries or hangings or a display of the glittering gold and silver plate that travelled with the king or queen.

After Queen Philippa's death in 1369, the royal household was often based in the grand new lodgings at Windsor, while Edward III himself visited the castle more rarely, preferring to travel with a smaller entourage to his other residences while the government was increasingly controlled by a small clique of courtiers. The Black Prince died in 1376, and Edward III the following year, leaving the throne to another boy, the Black Prince's ten-year-old son, Richard II.

Richard grew up to become a great artistic patron, but Edward III's alterations at Windsor were too recently completed for him to need to make many lasting changes to the castle. It remained an important residence though, and a useful refuge during outbreaks of plague. After he attained his majority, Richard's style of government was increasingly despotic, and having alienated many of his most powerful nobles he was imprisoned at Pontefract Castle in Yorkshire and forced to abdicate on 29 September 1399. Henry Bolingbroke, son of Richard's uncle John of Gaunt, was crowned Henry IV, although he continued to face opposition from Richard's supporters. In an attempt to avert further challenges in support of Richard's heir, the young Edmund Mortimer, a great-grandson of Edward III, Henry had the boy and his brother brought up in captivity at Windsor.

The castle was home to other prisoners, too. In 1405 the young James I of Scotland was captured at sea while on his way to the French court. He was imprisoned and in 1413 was moved to Windsor Castle, where he was held for another 11 years. James received a good education at the English court and lived comfortably in one of the castle's towers. A poet, he wrote 'The Kingis Quair' about how he fell in love with a young woman walking in the 'gardyn faire' beneath his tower window. She was Joan Beaufort and Henry V's niece;

Edward III's private apartments were painted in rich colours and although the furniture was mostly portable, the rooms could be quickly transformed with splendid fabrics and displays of glittering plate. This reconstruction of the octagonal 'Painted Chamber' in the Rose Tower shows how it may have appeared around 1366, when it was used by Edward for intimate gatherings.

James married her after his release from captivity and shortly before his return to Scotland in 1424.

Henry V's French queen, Catherine of Valois, gave birth to the future Henry VI at Windsor in 1421, but the baby was not even a year old before his father died of dysentery in France. As soon as the news of Henry V's death reached England, a regency government was established and the royal councillors hurried to Windsor, where they delivered their great seals of office to the infant king in the Great Chamber.

Henry VI's reign was a long and often troubled one. Henry was famously pious, and in 1440 founded Eton College, which had an educational as well as a charitable and religious purpose, but his political,

great and ruinous decay

diplomatic and military efforts were less successful. His armies struggled to defend Henry V's conquests in France and the French Crown reconquered Normandy in 1450 and Gascony in 1453. The shame and disgrace caused Henry VI to suffer a complete breakdown. For 17 months he could not speak, recognise anyone or apparently understand anything, and he spent most of this time in seclusion at Windsor, much as George III did in the early nineteenth century. When Henry recovered he had no memory of the episode, but the political situation continued to spiral out of control as opposition to a government widely regarded as corrupt coalesced around Richard, Duke of York (his father's second cousin), and the country was once again torn apart by the bitter civil war that later became known as the Wars of the Roses.

After Richard's death in battle in 1460, the conflict led to the bloody Battle of Towton the following year. Henry VI's forces were defeated, the king went into hiding, and the Duke of York's 18-year-old son was proclaimed King Edward IV by his followers. Henry VI was restored briefly to the throne in 1470–1, but Edward soon resumed power and the old king was murdered.

By this time Windsor Castle had been neglected for some years. An account of 1457 noted that the roof was leaking in many places and that the castle had fallen into 'great and ruinous decay'. Planning a Yorkist dynasty, Edward IV decided on Windsor as a place of burial and it was he who started building St George's Chapel next to Henry III's Great Chapel (see St George's Chapel, pp. 56–61). He

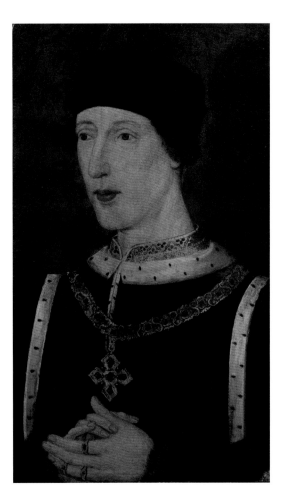

Portrait of Henry VI by an anonymous artist, *c*.1504–20

A pious but politically inept king, Henry VI (1421–71) spent much of his time secluded at Windsor while his Lancastrian supporters fought the Yorkist Edward IV.

Conjectural reconstruction of the Great Chamber during preparations for the Garter feast held there on 28 April 1476.

refurbished the dilapidated royal lodgings at the same time, and when the Duke of Burgundy's ambassador visited Windsor in 1472, they were once more fit for entertaining in lavish style. The ambassador, Seigneur de la Gruthuyse, was entertained in the queen's chamber, where the king danced with his eldest daughter, Elizabeth. The following day there was hunting and a tour of the garden before evensong. Later the queen hosted a banquet in her chamber, after which Elizabeth accompanied the ambassador to his rooms, which were hung with white silk and linen cloth, and the floor covered

with carpets. His bed had fine sheets and a coverlet furred with ermine, while the tester was made of shining cloth of gold and the curtains of fine white silk sarsenet.

Windsor was one of Edward IV's favourite residences, but his brother Richard III, who succeeded him in 1483, spent little time at the castle, and after Richard's defeat and death at the Battle of Bosworth Field in 1485, Windsor passed to the Tudors.

GUARDING THE CASTLE

Founded as a military garrison by William the Conqueror, Windsor Castle's first occupants were soldiers. They may have been mercenaries, or part of the contingents of men-at-arms from Brittany, Flanders and France who had joined those from Normandy in the invasion. The simple motte and bailey design favoured by the Normans made their castles quick to construct and easily defensible. They allowed William to establish fortified bases from which to dominate the surrounding countryside and crush the persistent rebellion that simmered for two decades after the Conquest. He 'built castles far and wide throughout the land', lamented the *Anglo-Saxon Chronicle*, 'oppressing the unhappy people, and things went ever from bad to worse'.

As the Normans consolidated control in England, the continuing defence of Windsor Castle was met by the payment of 'scutage' or 'shield-service'. The Norman kings rewarded their supporters with land, but ownership came with strings attached. Land was granted 'in fee' to tenants-in-chief such as barons, bishops and monasteries. They in turn divided their estates into 'knights' fees', a fee being a manor, or part of one, whose revenue was sufficient to support one knight with his horse and equipment for a fixed period of service, and the fees were then let to sub-tenants. These were usually men of knightly rank who were either expected to perform military service for the king themselves, or pay someone else to do it on their behalf. By the reign of Henry I, that military service

Above: Troops from all three of the Armed Services took part in a Diamond Jubilee Parade and Muster in front of The Queen at Windsor Castle in 2012, continuing a tradition of impressive military displays in the Quadrangle that dates back to the time of Edward III.

Opposite: Changing the Guard

The privilege of guarding the monarch traditionally belongs to the troops of the Household Division, better known as the Guards, who have carried out this duty since the regiments were formed as part of Britain's first standing army in 1660.

was more usually commuted to a monetary payment, or 'scutage'.

In the twelfth century 'scutage' was calculated at £1 a year and covered at least some of the expenses of 'castle-guard'. Some 73 baronies, collectively referred to as the 'Honour of Windsor', supported the garrison at Windsor Castle, thus bringing in £73 a year in 'castle-guard' dues. This provided four shillings a day, or enough to pay the six knights who formed the core of the castle's garrison, although probably not to cover the costs of maintaining the castle defences or supporting all the other people required to run the castle, such as men-at-arms, grooms, watchmen, servants and so on. The castle itself was under the command of the Constable; the knights and men who formed

the first garrisons at Windsor were there not only to defend the castle for the king but also to police the forest, administer justice and enforce the collection of revenues.

Windsor remained garrisoned with troops holding the castle on behalf of the monarch until the Civil War, when it was occupied by the New Model Army for Parliament until the Restoration of the monarchy. It was Charles II who first created a standing army. The original regiments were drawn not only from those who had fought on the Royalist side but also from the New Model Army, which had an impressive reputation for discipline. The Household Troops, better known as 'the Guards', were formed as part of that army. The Guards consist of five infantry regiments – the Grenadier,

Coldstream, Scots, Irish and Welsh Guards – known as the Household Division, and two regiments of the Household Cavalry, the Life Guards and the Blues and Royals. Today these regiments retain their traditional privilege of guarding the sovereign at Windsor Castle, although occasionally the honour will be extended to other regiments or to one of the other Armed Services: in November 2017 Windsor Castle was guarded for the first time by the Royal Navy.

The Windsor Castle Guard is sometimes provided by one of the five regiments of Foot Guards from the Household Division, instantly recognisable in their bearskin caps and scarlet tunics. The Guard is changed in a colourful ceremony that marks the handover of duties between two groups of Guards. Changing the Guard, also known as 'Guard Mounting', begins with the Windsor Castle Guard, who form up outside the Guard Room in the Lower Ward. The new Guard marches from Victoria Barracks in Windsor town, and are led by a Regimental Band, Corps of Drums or occasionally a Pipe Band. They arrive in the Lower Ward for a 45-minute ceremony during which the sentries change and duties are handed over. The old Guard then marches back to the barracks.

The ceremony marks a long tradition of guarding the castle for the monarch, but it is more than mere spectacle. The soldiers are on active duty, and when not guarding Windsor Castle may be serving overseas, sometimes in some of the more dangerous parts of the world.

The old Guard forming up outside the Guard Room in the Lower Ward during the Changing the Guard.

THE ORDER OF THE GARTER

Inspired by tales of the legendary King Arthur and the Knights of the Round Table, Edward III created a new order drawing on Arthurian ideals of chivalry, honour and knightly prowess. He envisaged a knightly elite, a fraternity fiercely loyal to the monarch and a highly trained band of warriors who would be able to support him in his ambition to reclaim his ancestral lands in Aquitaine and Gascony and in his claim to the French Crown itself.

Edward's first attempt to found an Order of the Round Table came to nothing, probably due to lack of money, but after his spectacular success at the battle of Crécy in August 1346, when the French army was routed, he returned to the idea of a chivalric order. The establishment of the new Order of the Garter was conceived not only as a reward for those who had fought with him and his heir, the Black Prince, at Crécy, but also as a symbol of his claim to the French Crown. The Order's motto, *Honi soit qui mal y pense* ('shame on him who thinks evil of it'), probably referred to this claim, condemning all those who questioned it.

Why the garter was chosen as a device for the new company remains unclear. Legend has it that when Joan of Kent, the Black Prince's wife, lost her garter while dancing, it was gallantly retrieved by Edward III. But the more likely, if less romantic, explanation lies in the military background to the Order. A garter – a strap used to bind pieces of armour together – had been used on pennons and streamers during the Crécy campaign and it may have been considered symbolic.

Left: Detail of the Garter star.

Edward's new Order consisted of 24 companion knights loyal to the king as sovereign or superior of the Order, and to his son, the Black Prince. The founder knights were drawn principally from the ranks of those who had contributed to the victory

Above: Gold and enamel badge of the Order of the Garter, 1775–1800

The badge is inscribed with the motto of the Order, *Honi soit qui mal y pense.*

Right: Stall plates in the quire stalls of St George's Chapel

The earliest stall plate, of the 44th Knight, Ralph, Lord Basset, is at top centre and was made about 1390. Added to with the election of each new knight since the sixteenth century, the collection of stall plates now numbers almost 800 and forms a unique assemblage of heraldic art.

Above: Garter star

Made of diamonds, rubies, enamel, silver and gold, the star badge was added to the Garter insignia by Charles I.

Above right: The Queen in Garter robes, photographed by Cecil Beaton, November 1955.

at Crécy, and were chosen on the basis of personal worthiness, martial renown and unblemished reputations. It is likely that the statutes were issued and the first companion knights were inducted to the new Order in 1348, which is widely accepted as the foundation year for the Order of the Garter, while the tournament held at Windsor on 23 April 1349 may have served as the first gathering of members of the Order.

The choice of St George's feast day for the tournament was significant. Edward III had dropped the emphasis on King Arthur and chose instead St George as patron saint of the Order. The patron saint of soldiers as well as of England, St George was a suitably martial figure, and has been closely associated with Windsor Castle ever since.

Each year on St George's Day, the Sovereign and Knight Companions of the Order of the Garter gathered for a great feast and often a tournament, which usually took place at Windsor Castle but could be held in any of the royal palaces where the monarch was residing. Any new Knight Companions were invested with their Garter robes and regalia on Garter Day, wherever it was celebrated. However, installation – the ceremony by which new Garter Knights were presented to their stalls – could only take place at Windsor, where the stalls were located.

Almost 700 years later, the Order of the

Wearing the Garter robes and insignia, The Queen walks in procession with The Prince of Wales and The Duke of Cambridge in the annual Garter Ceremony, 17 June 2013.

Garter is the oldest and most senior order of chivalry in Britain and many of its traditions continue. As monarch, The Queen is Sovereign of the Order. The Prince of Wales also forms part of the Companionship of 26, and a number of other senior members of the Royal Family are also Knights, or, in the case of female members of the British Royal Family, Ladies of the Order of the Garter. Male foreign monarchs invited to join the Order are known as Stranger Knights; female monarchs as Extra Ladies of the Order of the Garter. They currently include the Queen of Denmark and the kings of Spain, Sweden and Norway. Knight or Lady Companions are chosen personally by the Sovereign, to honour those who have distinguished themselves in the service of the nation or who have served the Sovereign personally.

Today the Garter Day procession takes place in June, rather than on 23 April. The Queen and members of the Order wear the distinctive Garter robes, their velvet cloaks, glistening insignia and ostrich-plumed hats. Accompanied by a marching band, they process on foot from the State Apartments to St George's Chapel for a short service before returning to the Upper Ward in horse-drawn carriages.

2

THE TUDOR AND EARLY STUART CASTLE

The early years of Henry VII's reign were spent away from Windsor, and included both his coronation and his marriage – in January 1485 – to Edward IV's daughter, Elizabeth of York. It was not until January 1487 that Henry first came to Windsor and he found the royal lodgings essentially unchanged since the time of Edward III, his great-great-great-grandfather. The rooms had been designed to be used flexibly, their size and space conveying a sense of magnificence and grandeur while changes in fashion were signalled by new hangings, furniture or the display of precious objects. In spite of their age, the apartments still provided an appropriate backdrop when the king took the whole court to Windsor for Easter 1488. Indeed, the very antiquity of the castle and its furnishings was appealing to Henry, who deliberately left the royal apartments

unmodernised and ordered the hanging of
ancient tapestries to underline his connection
to his illustrious ancestor, Edward III, from
whom his wife was also directly descended.
While other royal palaces were brought up to
date, Windsor was kept largely as it was, the
ultimate expression of antique courtly chivalry.

In 1488, therefore, a programme was
created to present Henry VII in splendour,
and a magnificent procession was planned
for Easter Sunday. The king wore purple
robes and was accompanied by the queen,
his mother, Lady Margaret Beaufort, and
the cream of the nobility. St George's Day
that year fell on a Wednesday. The royal
family, key advisers in the new regime and
the Garter Knights heard Mass in the king's
private chapel and dined in the intimate
surroundings of the Rose Tower. The Garter
feast itself was held that Sunday (27 April,
three weeks after Easter) in St George's Hall.

In spite of the confident display of
authority, Henry VII's claim to the throne
remained tenuous, and he lived in fear of
treacherous advisers and rival claimants

*The Yeomen of the
Guard form the end
of a procession in the
Quadrangle, accompanying
the monarch as they have
done since the fifteenth
century.*

*elaborate ceilings, fireplaces
finely carved with portcullises,
Tudor roses and fleurs-de-lis,
and tapestries on the walls*

around whom support might easily gather.
Obsessed with his personal security, he
created a new bodyguard, the Yeomen of
the Guard, to protect the monarch in his
own palaces and to control access through
the outer chambers. For the Easter Court in
1488, almost all the locks in the Upper Ward
were replaced, and new keys cut and issued
only to those authorised to have them.

After his Lord Chamberlain and Lord
Steward were accused of treason in 1493,
Henry went further, creating a new
department of the royal household. The
Privy Chamber, serving the personal needs
of the king, was staffed not by ambitious
nobles but by those whose lack of social status
meant that he could rely on their loyalty.
The most intimate access to the king now lay
not with the nobility but with a few grooms
under the Groom of the Stool, who had the
unenviable honour of assisting the king with
his excretions and ablutions, but who held as
a result an extremely powerful position.

Henry VII's preoccupation with security led
to the commission of a new three-storey tower
in the Upper Ward as an inner sanctum for
the king. The rooms, elements of which still
survive (now occupied by the Royal Library),
were small but beautifully decorated. There
were elaborate ceilings, fireplaces finely
carved with portcullises, Tudor roses and
fleurs-de-lis, and tapestries on the walls.
With the woodwork and stonework painted
and gilded, and a guard at the foot of the

stairs, it must have been a luxurious retreat for the king. These were the most private of the king's rooms, his bedchamber, closet for study and his personal library, which was probably on the top floor, far from any damp and where there was good light.

The king's official lodging as described during the King of Castile's visit in 1506 consisted of a Great Chamber, a second chamber and a Chamber of Estate, or dining chamber. Access to the monarch was carefully controlled according to status. Knights and esquires waited in the first room, barons in

Above: Ever anxious about security, Henry VII promoted a number of humbly born advisers who would owe their loyalty to him rather than to a noble family. One such person was Sir Reginald Bray, who was made a Knight of the Garter in 1501, thanks to the king's patronage. Bray donated a considerable part of his large fortune to pay for the completion of the nave of St George's Chapel, and his generosity was marked by the inclusion of his heraldic badge, a hemp-bray, no less than 175 times in the chapel's interior. A toothed device for crushing hemp, the hemp-bray was both a pun on his name and a reflection of his lowly origins.

MARCI 16
ITE IN MVVVM VNIVERSV ET PREDICATE
EVANGELIVM OMNI CREATVRE

the second and bishops and earls in the third, which was furnished with a canopy of state and a state bed, a symbolic piece of furniture rather than somewhere to sleep. The rooms were decorated with progressive elaboration. The innermost, or Privy Chamber, where only those of the highest status had direct access to the king, was hung with cloth of gold bordered with crimson velvet.

In spite of his new tower, Henry VII spent little time at Windsor, but he was a shrewd supporter of the Order of the Garter, using the patronage it offered to strengthen his position as King and to bring together men of different backgrounds – the old nobility and humbly born advisers – uniting them in shared vows of loyalty to the Order and to the Sovereign. It was Henry who strengthened the oaths taken by new knights, who in addition to the traditional vow to support and defend the Order now also promised to 'defend and uphold the honours, causes, rights and lordships of the Sovereign of the

Order'. Henry also made diplomatic use of the Order's prestigious reputation: the kings of Portugal, Denmark and Castile were all appointed to the Order, together with the future Emperor Maximilian I. He was, too, the last monarch for 400 years to award the Garter to a lady. His mother, Lady Margaret Beaufort, and his two daughters, Margaret and Elizabeth, were received into the Order, following a tradition begun in the fourteenth century which allowed female relatives and friends to be associated members, who could therefore share in the ceremonies and feasting. The practice was abandoned by Henry VIII and it was not until 1901 that King Edward VII decided to revive the custom by appointing Queen Alexandra as a Lady of the Garter.

Henry VIII had been appointed a Knight of the Garter in 1495, when he was still Duke of York. The pomp and ceremony associated with the Order appealed to him and he took a great interest in it, drawing up revised

Left: Henry VIII, by Joos van Cleve (1485–1541), *c.*1530–5

Once described by the Venetian Ambassador as 'the best dressed sovereign in the world', Henry VIII (1491–1547) wore richly coloured clothes adorned with jewels and furs to convey the magnificence of the Tudor monarchy.

Right: Henry VIII with the Knights of the Garter, from the Black Book of the Garter, *c.*1534

This beautifully illuminated register may have been commissioned by Henry after drawing up revised statutes for the Order of the Garter.

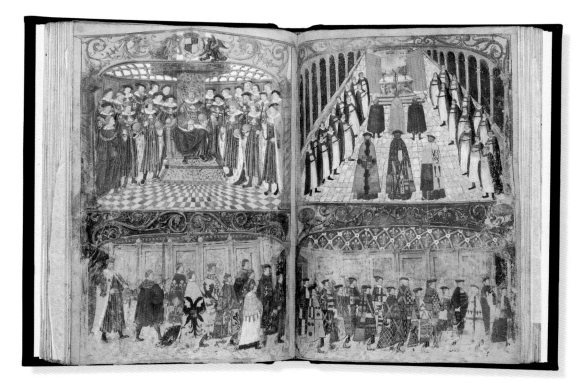

statutes; it may have been Henry VIII himself who commissioned a new and beautifully illuminated Garter register, the Black Book of the Garter. However, many of the Garter activities now tended to be held wherever the king happened to be. Although the annual St George's Day feast and installations continued at Windsor Castle, the king himself was often absent, appointing instead a deputy from among the Garter Knights to represent him.

At other times Henry VIII came regularly to the castle. He preferred to visit later in the year, in July and August for hunting and hawking in Windsor's parks and forest, and returning for the deer-hunting season in October and November. Henry VIII was a keen hunter and sportsman, and as a young man had apparently boundless energy: 'His Grace, euery after noone, when the wether ys any thing feyer, dooth ride ffurthe on hawking, or walkyth in the Parke, and cummyth not inne ageyne till yt be late in the evenyng', wrote Thomas Heneage from Windsor in 1527.

The superb hunting at Windsor was offered as an honour to important visitors and played a role in diplomacy. Emperor Charles V was entertained at the castle in 1522 and spent three days hunting with Henry, while Frederick, Duke of Bavaria, and Frederick,

Prince Elector of Saxony, had eight days of hunting and feasting in September 1539. Ambassadors came out to Windsor too, in the hope of being afforded the privilege of hunting with the king.

Henry VIII did little modernising at Windsor Castle. Like his father, he used the imposing antiquity of the castle to deliberate effect and kept the old tapestries and other furnishings in place. When hunting, he often stayed at smaller houses within the forest with close friends, leaving the full court at the castle. However, a new gate that bears his name was constructed in the Lower Ward, and, most importantly, he ordered the construction of a terrace along the north side of the castle. The king's 'New Walk' was made of timber and raised on brick vaults that served as water tanks, storing the run-off from the lead roofs. A bridge at the east end spanned the castle ditch and gave access to the Little Park. The terrace gave a domestic feel to the castle, and reflected a new sense of security in Henry's reign.

On 24 October 1537 Henry VIII's third wife, Jane Seymour, died at Hampton Court, 12 days after giving birth to a much longed-for son, the future Edward VI. A small brick vault was created in the middle of the quire in St George's Chapel, and the queen was

Henry VIII enjoyed the superb hunting at Windsor. His hunting sword and knife were made in 1544 by Diego de Çaias (active c.1535–52) and are now on display at Windsor Castle.

The arms of Mary I and her husband, Philip II of Spain, on the Mary Tudor Tower in the Lower Ward.

buried there on 12 November. Henry VII had a funerary monument in the magnificent chapel he had built in Westminster Abbey, but evidently his son had not decided on his own resting place. Various plans for suitable grand tombs were made during Henry VIII's reign, but in the event a spectacular funeral Mass was held in St George's Chapel after his death in 1547 and he was buried in the vault beside Queen Jane.

Edward VI was on the throne for too short a time to make much mark on the castle, and in any case disliked staying at Windsor. 'Methinks I am in a prison', he grumbled, 'here be no galleries nor no gardens to walk in.' During his reign work started to supplement the water supply provided by the water tanks under Henry VIII's wooden terrace. Fed by gravity, a conduit of lead piping emerged in an imposing fountain, created in Mary I's reign, in the middle of the Upper Ward, where the water settled in tanks before being piped around the castle.

Edward's successor, Mary I, had her husband, Philip II of Spain, installed as joint Sovereign of the Order of the Garter. It was she who arranged for almshouses to be constructed in the Lower Ward to accommodate the increasing number of veteran soldiers appointed as Poor Knights (known since 1833 as Military Knights). Seven houses were converted from existing buildings, while six new ones were added, with a common hall and kitchen. The central tower, once a belfry, was renovated and decorated with the arms of Mary and Philip. Now known as the Mary Tudor Tower, it is still occupied by the Governor of the Military Knights.

On Mary's death in 1558, the Crown passed to her half-sister, Elizabeth I. Like her father, Elizabeth loved hunting and Windsor was one of her favourite residences. She often stayed at the castle at the end of the summer, when she would ride out tirelessly, leaving her courtiers trailing behind. As the Spanish ambassador observed, 'she went so hard that

Elizabeth I when a Princess, attributed to William Scrots (active 1537–53), *c.*1546

This portrait of Princess Elizabeth, later Elizabeth I, shows her as a young girl in a crimson silk gown. The jewels and rich fabrics emphasise her beauty and dignity, while the book she carries indicates her learning. Elizabeth spoke Latin, Italian, French and Spanish, and after her accession her tutor continued to visit her at Windsor to read Greek and Latin texts with her.

it much misliketh her not to go somewhere to have change of air

one place. Windsor was a convenient refuge whenever plague made London dangerous, but Elizabeth was often fretful. '[We] all do what we can to persuade from any progress at all, only to remain at Windsor, and thereabouts', Leicester wrote with a trace of weariness in 1577. 'But it much misliketh her not to go somewhere to have change of air.'

Elizabeth followed the precedent set by Mary I and took over the 'king's' apartments in all 45 of her residences, including Windsor. As a woman, her inner chamber was staffed by females, who provided personal service and slept in her bedchamber and privy chamber next door. Much as her grandfather, Henry VII, had established, Elizabeth's Privy Chamber served more as a domestic support system than a focus of political manoeuvring. Private her inner chambers may have been, but Elizabeth perfectly understood the importance of ceremonial and the etiquette of the court, which reinforced her regal authority.

she tired everybody out, and as the ladies and courtiers were with her they were all put to shame. There was more work than pleasure in it for them'.

Often Elizabeth would ride out with her favourite, Robert Dudley, Earl of Leicester. A brilliant horseman, he was given two key posts in the queen's household, Master of the Horse and Master of the Royal Buckhounds, which put him in charge of her transport and hunting and ensured that he was by her side almost continuously. The queen also appointed him Constable of Windsor Castle and Keeper of the Great Park. In addition, it was up to Leicester to calm a restless queen when she grew frustrated by enforced stays in

Although in general Elizabeth left it to her courtiers to build lavishly to entertain her, she did make two important additions to Windsor Castle. The first was to replace Henry VIII's timber walkway with what is now the North Terrace. The responsibility for getting the work done was handed to an administrator called Humphrey Mitchell. Poor Mitchell had to cope with the queen, the Earl of Leicester and the queen's powerful Secretary, Sir William Cecil, all with their own opinions and a tiresome propensity to change their minds. Mitchell's first attempt at a plain retaining wall with a parapet met with a barrage of criticism and he was ordered to extend the terrace and replace the parapet

Elizabeth I commissioned the North Terrace to replace
Henry VIII's timber walkway. The queen changed her
mind about the design so often that the official charged
with completing the project tried to resign on being told
that the work was still 'not pleasing or acceptable to our
lady the queen'.

One of the most beautiful stone chimney-pieces of the age, the elaborately carved fireplace in Elizabeth I's gallery was made to celebrate her 50th birthday in 1583. The fireplace is carved with a number of symbols of particular significance to Elizabeth, as well as with heraldic beasts, including the dragon, the greyhound and the antelope shown in the detail.

with balusters, buttresses and built-in stone seats, as well as building a bridge into the park at the east end. The terrace cost more than £1,000, and when Mitchell was told that the work was still 'not pleasing or acceptable to our lady the queen', he tried to resign. As Constable, Leicester refused to accept his resignation but did appoint a surveyor or architect, Henry Hawthorne, to work alongside him. When the North Terrace was completed, and Elizabeth decided that she would have a gallery and a banqueting house

built, Mitchell wrote to Cecil begging him to ensure that Hawthorne draw up precise plans in advance, 'that there may not be any alteration after they are set up, for I have found by experience (by doing and undoing) things have grown very chargeable'.

Elizabeth's gallery at Windsor Castle, which bears her ER monogram and the date, 1583, is located to the north west of the Upper Ward and is one of her most important works. A gallery was by this time one of the fundamental components of a sovereign's private, or privy, apartments, together with a bedchamber and a closet, used for private study. The entrance to the gallery was through her bedchamber (in Henry VII's tower), and the original plan was to link the queen's lodgings with those of Leicester, her close companion, who as Constable resided in the Norman Gate when at Windsor. But Leicester died in 1588 before the gallery was completed and the link between the two buildings was never made.

From the gallery, a stair led down to an ante-room with a door into the courtyard, which probably became the queen's main entrance to her lodgings. The stair continued down to another door that opened onto the North Terrace, where she could walk or ride out into the park. A covered area at the foot of the stairs meant that she could mount her horse in the dry when it was raining.

A bird's-eye view of Windsor Castle from *A Description of the Honor of Windesor*, by John Norden (*c.*1547–1625), 1607

Prepared for James I, Norden's view shows St George's Chapel on the right, Elizabeth I's new terrace leading to Little Park on the left and paths criss-crossing the Upper Ward. The fountain in the middle of what is now the Quadrangle was created in the reign of Mary I (1516–58). Water conduits led to the fountain, where it settled in tanks before being piped around the castle.

Elizabeth famously took 'great Delight in being out in the Air', but was said to have hated 'to be russled by the wind'.

The gallery itself has an elaborate plaster ceiling and a beautifully carved stone fireplace, which was made to celebrate Elizabeth's 50th birthday in 1583 and incorporates many symbols of particular significance to her, including the coat of arms of her mother, Anne Boleyn. Because it was a primarily female space, few men were allowed inside, and only under tightly controlled circumstances. We do not have many descriptions of exactly how the gallery was used, but according to the observant Baron Waldstein, who managed to get a glimpse inside, there was a couch on which Elizabeth sat when consulting with her ministers, and it is likely that the room would have been a place of recreation and study as well as business. Roger Ascham, Elizabeth's former tutor, went to Windsor to read Greek and Latin texts with the queen after her accession: 'beside her perfect readiness in Latin, Italian, French and Spanish', he claimed,

she readeth now here at Windsor more Greek every day than some prebendary of this church doth read Latin in a whole week

'she readeth now here at Windsor more Greek every day than some prebendary of this church doth read Latin in a whole week'. Reading and study of this kind probably took place in the gallery, which was designed to be long enough for the queen and her ladies to walk up and down when the weather was too bad for even Elizabeth to want to go out.

James VI of Scotland received news of Elizabeth's death and his own succession as James I of England on 26 March 1603. Setting off for London, he found the capital in the grip of an epidemic of plague and was advised to move west to Windsor instead. On his arrival James inspected the castle, and was so pleased with what he saw that he decreed that his family should gather

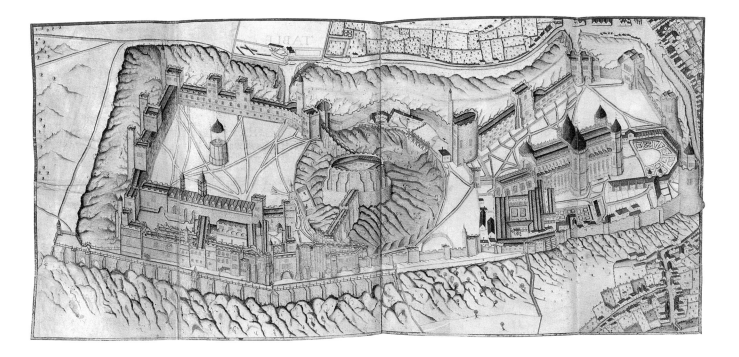

Charles I and Henrietta Maria, by Daniel Mytens (1590–1647), *c.*1630–2
This unusual double portrait depicts Charles I (1600–49) and his young queen. The daughter of Henri IV of France, Henrietta Maria (1609–69) offers Charles a laurel wreath as a symbol of their union and a public statement of tenderness and intimacy.

there. Accordingly, he met his queen, Anne of Denmark, at Towcester on 27 June and escorted her and their eldest son, Henry, directly to Windsor where their daughter, Elizabeth, was waiting. It was at Windsor Castle, therefore, that the Scottish and English courts first came together and took stock of each other. 'We were much troubled here with certain wrangling Scots who, wheresoever they came, would have meat, drink, and lodging by strong hand', wrote

---

We were much troubled here with certain wrangling Scots

---

one English observer, unimpressed. He also described the new king's irritation after his wife had better luck when out hunting: 'in the afternoon she killed a buck out of standing, at which the king was so angry and discontented that she returned home without his company'.

On later occasions James had more luck, and he was a regular visitor to Windsor Castle to enjoy the excellent hunting in the forest. A poetic description of 1612 associated castle and forest as 'that supremest place of the great English kings' and James certainly made good use of both. In most years he would make a short visit in June or July before setting out on the annual summer progress around the country and returning to Windsor in August or September, when he 'ended his summer hunting'. He then met the queen at Hampton Court and they moved together to Whitehall Palace for the winter season.

Charles I's associations with Windsor Castle were less happy. His older brother, Henry, died in 1612 and so it was Charles who became king on James's death in 1625. Charles revelled in the historical, military, chivalrous and spiritual associations of the Order of the Garter, but for the first few years of his reign he was only an occasional visitor.

The court did move to the castle in the summer of 1636, to avoid the plague that was particularly severe in London that year, and when tensions between the Crown and Parliament came to a head in January 1642 Charles fled to Windsor once more, this time not in fear of disease but in the hope that it would keep him 'secure from any sudden popular attempt'. For a month he remained at the castle negotiating with Parliament. Members of both Houses of Parliament came to Windsor to present a petition demanding that the Tower of London and the 'militia of the kingdom' be placed under

Watercolour by Alfred Young Nutt (1847–1924) of the vault below the quire of St George's Chapel, with the coffins of Charles I, Henry VIII, Jane Seymour and an unnamed child of Queen Anne. Nutt made this watercolour, with a plan, on the opening of the vault on 13 December 1888.

the cook disappointed him of mince pie and plum porridge

parliamentary control. The king prevaricated, but rumours that a thousand Londoners were marching on the castle with further petitions meant that Windsor felt less safe, and on 10 February 1642 Charles's court left Windsor for the last time.

In spite of its close connection with the castle, the town of Windsor was staunchly Puritan and sided with Parliament from the start of the conflict. For perhaps the first time in its long history, the castle was left ungarrisoned until October 1642, when Parliament decided that 'some especial care' should be taken of it. On 28 October a Parliamentary force occupied Windsor Castle, and for the rest of the Civil War it remained under Parliamentary control. For much of the time, indeed, it was effectively the headquarters of the Parliamentary army and Oliver Cromwell often visited, particularly once Charles I had been captured in 1647 and while negotiations about his trial were taking place.

Charles was returned to the castle for a brief visit soon after his capture but then taken on to Caversham. In December 1648 he was sent back to Windsor, where he was greeted at the castle gate by a kneeling Duke of Hamilton, once his chief supporter in Scotland and by then also a prisoner. The king and his attendants were given an allowance of £15 a day. The castle was ordered to be emptied of 'all malignant and Cavalierish inhabitants' who might dare to sympathise with the king, but Charles took the poor fare with good grace: 'though the cook disappointed him of mince pie and plum porridge, yet he resolved to keep Christmas, and accordingly put on his best

The Burial of Charles I at Windsor, by Charles West Cope (1811–90), 1861

This mural decoration for the Peers' Corridor of the Palace of Westminster shows Charles I's coffin being carried into St George's Chapel in the middle of a snowstorm, while the Bishop of London is refused permission to use the Book of Common Prayer for the service.

clothes, and himself is chaplain that attend him, reading and expanding the scripture to them.'

On 19 January 1649 Charles was taken to St James's Palace. He was tried in Westminster Hall and executed outside the Banqueting House in Whitehall on 30 January. Parliament ordered that he be buried at Windsor, provided that expenses did not exceed £500. His body was taken to Windsor on 7 February and his coffin placed in the king's bedchamber overnight. Four of Charles I's officers of the bedchamber had requested permission 'to perform the last duty to their dead master, and to wait upon him to his grave', but no appropriate burial place had been identified in St George's Chapel. With the help of

in silence and sorrow

one of the old Poor Knights they searched the chapel, tapping on the floor until they located an unmarked vault. When opened, they found that it contained the coffins of Henry VIII and Jane Seymour. The following day, 9 February 1649, the king's coffin was covered with a black velvet pall and carried into the chapel, but it was snowing so hard that the snow turned the black pall white, which Royalists interpreted as a sign of the king's innocence. The Bishop of London was in attendance, but his request to use the Book of Common Prayer for the service was brusquely refused and Charles I was buried without a service, 'in silence and sorrow'. The burial was recorded in the town's parish register.

After the king's execution, his extraordinary collection of art, consisting of an estimated 1,500 paintings and

500 sculptures, was sold by Cromwell's government, which wanted to pay off the dead king's debts and to raise money for the state. Works of art were handed over in part payment for money owed for palace repairs. John Embry, a plumber, was owed £903, a huge amount of money. Plumbers at the time were responsible for most of the lead works on a building site, and Embry seems to have had a substantial business. The government offered him a deal to settle the debt: £403 in cash and the balance to be made up with pictures. Embry chose 24 paintings, including one by Titian, valued then at £100.

For much of the Civil War and until the end of the Commonwealth, Windsor Castle was used as a prison. Prisoners of higher rank were expected to pay a weekly allowance, and although they were not allowed to leave the castle, speak to visitors or send or receive letters, their existence may not have been too uncomfortable. Such prisoners were lodged in the Poor Knights' houses, the Henry VIII Gate and various towers, as well as the Norman Gate, where some finely carved graffiti by Royalist prisoners can still be seen in the first-floor room.

Life was grimmer for other, lower-ranking prisoners, who were kept in the large basement vault of Curfew Tower. An account of 1643 describes how the prisoners were locked into 'close, stinking dungeons' and allowed only five farthings a day in bread and water, 'into which it is more than probable that some poison was put, for eight captains and gentlemen of good worth died within this fortnight, many of them being well overnight and dead the next day'.

Windsor Castle remained an important garrison under the Commonwealth, but catastrophe was only narrowly averted in November 1652 when the Commons resolved that 'the castle of Windsore, with all the House, Parks and Lands there, belonging to the State, be sold for ready money'. The proposition was debated on 29 December and defeated by 29 votes to 19, although the Great and Little Parks were divided into plots and sold. In 1654, however, Cromwell ordered that the Little Park be repurchased at a cost of £3,470 5s.

Its use as a prison and garrison meant that the castle continued to be a busy place, but after years of neglect its splendour had faded and it was shabby and down at heel. John Evelyn, visiting in June 1654, commented on the size of the castle, but the rooms, he said, were 'melancholy and of ancient magnificence'.

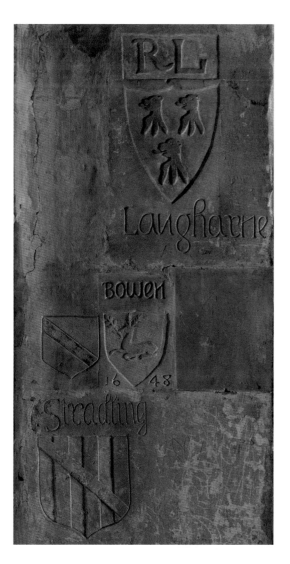

Graffiti carved by Royalist prisoners in the first-floor room of the Norman Gate, c.1642.

FEEDING THE CASTLE

Keeping Windsor Castle provisioned and its occupants fed has been a challenge throughout its history. The logistics of sourcing, preparing, cooking and serving meals at the castle was in the earlier medieval period the responsibility of the Constable. Not only did he have to ensure that everyone from the monarch downwards was fed on a day-to-day basis, but he also had to provide meals on a spectacular scale. Feasting was an integral part of the exercise of kingship in the Middle Ages. It was a way of displaying the wealth and power of the sovereign; the more lavish the spread, the more extravagant and intricate the dishes, the greater the magnificence of the monarch was impressed upon those lucky enough to be seated at the table, or just able to watch the feast.

Edward III was well aware of the symbolic and political importance of feasting, and when he built his magnificent new palace in Upper Ward, he ensured that it was serviced by an equally magnificent kitchen. The two-storey Great Kitchen, still in use today, was lined with enormous fireplaces with spits for roasting and cauldrons for heating water. There was a separate bakehouse and various larders and storerooms, as well as the 'dressour', where dishes were prepared, the 'pasterye', a special area for desserts and confectionery, and the 'saucery', where sauces were made. Bread, beer and wine were stored and dispensed from the pantry and buttery, which was probably located at

the foot of the Great Stairs leading up to the Great Hall and the royal apartments.

At the beginning of the seventeenth century there were still a vast number of servants employed in what must have been a rabbit-warren of rooms attached to the Great Kitchen. Gifts or 'rewards' were distributed to mark New Year's Day and the records of who was given what in 1611 reveal a whole range of specialist jobs – the turnbroaches, who turned the spits; the scourbroaches, who had the unenviable task of cleaning the kitchen; the woodbearer, the sweeper, the glasser, the locksmith, the porters and 'the children of the Kitchen' – and almost as great a variety of spaces: the cellar, the buttery, the pantry and the pastery, all used as before, as well as the ewery, where the linen was kept, the scullery, the scalding-house, the boiling-house, the spicery, the saucer, the poultry, the timber yard and assorted larders.

Opposite: Decorative cake stand from the Rockingham Coronation Dessert Service holding a strawberry-topped Sablé Breton.

Below: A selection of jelly moulds from the reign of Queen Victoria. Her cipher can be seen branded into their rims.

Right: Mildred Nichols joined the royal household as seventh kitchen maid in 1908. Her recipe book contains numerous handwritten recipes for the cakes and puddings served to the royal family and to their servants while she was a pastry kitchen maid. These pages show different recipes for plum pudding, one to be served at the royal table and the other to the servants.

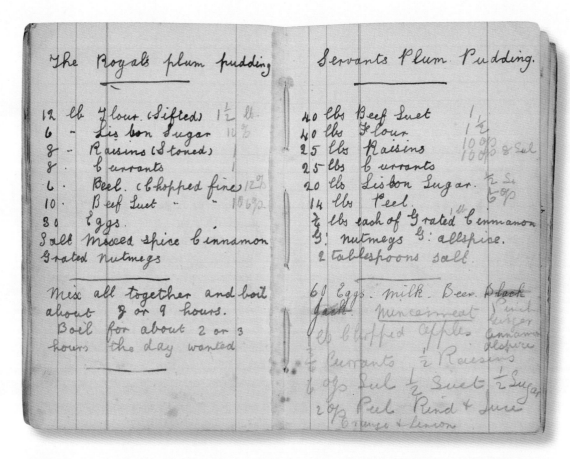

Charles II continued the tradition of eating in public. On these occasions he dined in solitary splendour under a canopy, watched from behind a balustrade by a crowd of interested spectators while musicians played. As in earlier times, the object of the exercise was to demonstrate the magnificence of the monarch, and he was served two courses of 29 dishes. The first course might include wild boar pie, haggis puddings and roasted pigs, while the second could offer anything from pickled oysters and pheasants served with their eggs to six roasted lobsters. The king took what he wanted and the remainder was distributed to the household or to the poor waiting at the castle gates.

By the time of Queen Victoria there were still a huge number of people entitled to be fed at royal expense. When the Queen was at Windsor, the royal kitchens had to provide meals for anything from a solitary lady-in-waiting lunching in her room to two sittings of a hundred people each in the Servants' Hall to a thousand guests at a buffet. This was catering on an industrial scale. The ledgers record that in March 1865, a typical month, the royal chefs supplied food for 8,257 people. Whether plain working-class fare, nursery food, a picnic for travellers, something to tempt the appetite of ailing royals or the most elaborate dishes designed to show off at a state banquet, the kitchen staff had to be able to provide it all.

At least by this time the Great Kitchen had been modernised as part of George IV's great remodelling of the Upper Ward. In addition, the walls had been lined with white tiles, the roof whitewashed and a stag's head mounted to oversee all the activity. More usefully, gas lighting had been installed and closed ranges filled four of the open hearths. There was hot water on demand from a cistern on the

Top: Chefs at work in the Great Kitchen.

Above: Making sauce in a copper saucepan, part of the extensive *batterie de cuisine* in the Great Kitchen.

roof, and a huge steam-heated steel table in the centre of the kitchen. There were chafing stoves and brick ovens and boiling coppers for large joints and puddings. There were turbot kettles, tiny dariole moulds, waffling irons, and a vast *batterie de cuisine* in copper, each piece crested and numbered, and still on display in the kitchen today. A confectionery, bakehouse and pastry room, each with its own staff, were fitted out to equally high standards with specialist equipment. The floors were spread with sand, which was replaced several times a day to ensure that all scraps and spills were removed efficiently.

One of Queen Victoria's dressers, Frieda

Arnold, visited the kitchen at Windsor Castle in 1855 and was suitably awed by the sheer size and scale of the operation:

There are twelve ranges, with a huge iron table in the centre which is heated from below, and on which the dishes are set. On both sides are huge fires over which roasts are suspended on spits, with great iron chains driven round constantly by a machine … But the greatest calm and order reigns, as if nothing was happening.

Much of the fresh produce came from the kitchen gardens and greenhouses at Frogmore House, which supplied huge quantities of vegetables to the castle kitchen. The kitchen garden books show that in 1869 16,800 bunches of carrots, 5,208 lb of old potatoes and 2,882 lb of new, 13,800 stalks of asparagus and 111 half-dozen beetroot were delivered to the kitchen, along with Jerusalem artichokes, rhubarb, cucumbers, endives, lettuces, radishes and other salad, and still additional produce had to be purchased to feed the hungry mouths at the castle.

Today the kitchen at Windsor continues to source as much as possible either locally or from other royal estates. As part of the Royal Household, the Royal Chef and his team move around with Her Majesty and, like their predecessors, provide meals for a wide variety of people and events. The most spectacular culinary occasions are the banquets laid on as part of a state visit. These are planned well in advance and the menus are approved personally by The Queen. The food preparation is timed with military precision. The finished plates are kept warm in warming ovens in the pantries behind St George's Hall, ready to be served by liveried footmen the moment the signal is given that the speeches are over and the guests are ready to eat.

Two-tier chocolate biscuit cake. The chocolate buttons were made using real footmen's buttons taken from Royal Household uniforms; these were used to create moulds into which melted dark and milk chocolate was poured. Some of the buttons were then brushed with gold-lustre dust to varying degrees, so that some appear completely gold and others merely glint.

THE COLLEGE OF ST GEORGE AND ST GEORGE'S CHAPEL

Christianity was integral to Edward III's vision of chivalry. In 1346 he founded the College of St George to act as the spiritual arm of the Order of the Garter and appointed a priestly body of 26 – a warden, 12 canons and 13 priest vicars – to mirror the assembly of 24 Knight Companions who, with the king and the Prince of Wales, made up the Order. Edward also planned the appointment of 24 impoverished army veterans, who would be responsible for praying for the Knights of the Garter on a daily basis, but until the Tudor period very few of these 'Poor Knights' (later known as Military Knights) seem to have been in place at any one time. The College was also served by four lay clerks (adult singers) and six boy choristers, besides a verger and two bell ringers.

Members of the College initially worshipped in Henry III's great chapel at Windsor, which was dedicated to the Blessed Virgin Mary and St Edward. Edward III rededicated the chapel to include St George, patron saint of the Order of the Garter, and it was not long before the chapel became known simply as St George's Chapel.

It was Edward IV who conceived the idea of a new chapel for the College. Edward visited Windsor in the autumn of 1471. Envisaging an ambitious chapel that would be a burial place for the Yorkist dynasty, Edward brought in Richard Beauchamp, Bishop of Salisbury and Chancellor of the Order of the Garter, to oversee its construction. Beauchamp was given *carte blanche* to clear the Lower Ward if necessary. The king took a close and personal interest in the project, and told the bishop 'to choose and take bricklayers, plumbers, carpenters, masons and other workmen and labourers' and 'to take and provide stones, timber, tiles, shingles, glass, iron, lead etc. necessary for the said works and to pay the carriage of them … also to make whatsoever payments there might be for the wages … and the purchase and carriage of materials'. As well as the chapel itself, accommodation was built for the lay clerks in what is now known as Horseshoe Cloister. While work was under way, the old chapel to the east continued to be used for services.

The new chapel was started in 1475 and was planned on the spectacular scale of a

Above: St George's Chapel from the south. Edward IV started building a new chapel at Windsor in 1475 but it was not completed until the reign of Henry VIII in 1528.

Far left: Detail of a boss in the crossing vault with the royal coat of arms.

Left: The misericords in the quire stalls were carved with a range of subjects both sacred and secular. These two show a game of backgammon (left) and a man supping with the Devil (right).

small cathedral. Edward III had presented the College with one of the most precious relics in the country, the 'Cross Gneth', a gold reliquary which was said to contain a fragment of the True Cross, and this was housed in the principal shrine at the east end of the new chapel.

Edward IV did not live to see his chapel completed. When he died in 1483, only the quire had been finished and roofed in timber, although it was already largely furnished with the magnificent wooden stalls that represent some of the most remarkable medieval carvings to survive anywhere in Europe. The ends of the stalls and the misericords were carved under the supervision of master woodcarver William Berkeley between 1478

and 1485 with a wealth of subjects ranging from the sacred to the comic.

The stalls themselves were originally intended to be allocated alternately to Garter Knights and canons, and as a result the canopies above were finished with different designs, pinnacles for canons and higher, tiered towers for knights. The knights' towers were topped with a series of carved wooden busts intended to 'wear' the individual knight's helm and crest, while the knights' banners were displayed above the stalls. The tradition of affixing an inscribed brass plate enamelled with a coat of arms to commemorate each Knight of the Garter after death had already been established in the old chapel, and when the stalls were

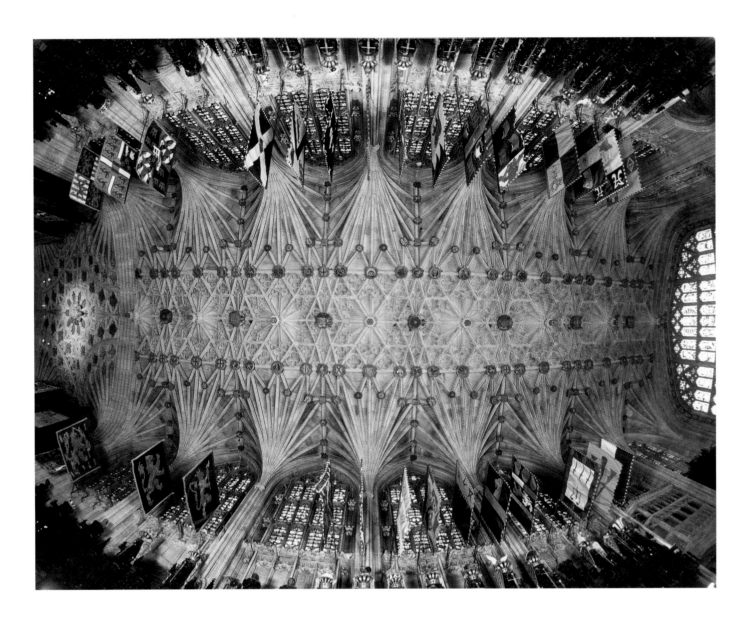

completed, the old stall plates were moved to the new chapel, beginning a sequence of more than 700 plates that together constitute a unique heraldic record from the fourteenth century to the twenty-first.

It was left to Henry VII, the first Tudor king, to take on the task of completing St George's Chapel. About eight years after his accession Henry decided to replace Henry III's chapel with a new Lady Chapel, which he originally intended to be his burial place. Building works began in 1494 but had not been completed by 1498, when Henry VII

abandoned the project in favour of constructing a Lady Chapel at the east end of Westminster Abbey, where he was buried after his death in 1509. The former Tomb House at Windsor was given a dramatic new interior in the nineteenth century, commissioned by Queen Victoria in memory of Prince Albert, and is now known as the Albert Memorial Chapel.

It was during the reign of Henry VII that the nave of St George's Chapel was completed with the exquisite fan vaulting, which is its most distinctive feature. The completion of the nave was financed by a

substantial bequest in the will of Sir Reginald Bray, a trusted servant of Henry VII who was elected to the Order of the Garter in 1501. Bray's personal device was a hemp-bray, which is featured in many places to reflect his generous contribution.

In 1506, on the completion of the nave vaulting, master stonemasons William Vertue and John Hylmer were engaged to install fan vaulting in the quire, the cost being met by contributions from the king and the Knights of the Garter. The original intention was to erect a tower and lantern over the crossing but the idea was given up, presumably because of the expense or for structural reasons. Instead the Knights of the Garter were asked for further donations to complete the final section of the vaulting during the reign of Henry VIII. This was finished in 1528, more than 50 years after the chapel was begun. The College's special status as a royal foundation saved it from dissolution at the Reformation, and St George's Chapel remains the glory of the medieval fabric of Windsor. With its large traceried windows, slender pillars and impression of soaring grace and elegance, it ranks as one of the finest examples of the Perpendicular style in Britain.

Today, St George's Chapel is a place of daily worship as it has always been, with services open to everyone. It is a Royal Peculiar, meaning that it is subject directly to the monarch and is not part of any diocese. The chapel continues to have a close association with the Royal Family, not only through the annual service of thanksgiving on Garter Day but also as the place where many family occasions are marked by a special service.

3

THE RESTORATION CASTLE

When Charles II returned to England in 1660 as king, he did so on a wave of popular support. The Protectorate established by Oliver Cromwell in 1653 had been a time of fervent Puritanism in England. Rigid social laws banned horse racing and cockfights, while plays were prohibited and many brothels, alehouses and gambling dens were closed in the name of public morality. Many of these measures had proved unpopular, however, and when Parliament offered to restore the monarchy there was widespread support for a move away from the severity of the previous years.

Charles II's reign certainly represented a change from austerity. Theatres were opened. There was dancing and music. The court was a byword for flamboyance and luxury and scandalous affairs openly pursued. Even today, Charles II is famous for his mistresses. But the transformation of Windsor Castle was about much more than overturning joyless social attitudes. Instead, the remodelling of the castle was deliberately designed to

provide a fitting backdrop to the rituals that reinforced the majesty of kingship.

For the restoration of the monarchy had come with strings attached. Parliament was fiercely Protestant while Charles, who was married to the Catholic Catherine of Braganza and whose brother, James, Duke of York, had converted to Catholicism, was in favour of greater toleration for Catholics. When Charles wanted funds to pursue a war against the Protestant Dutch, Parliament

a byword for flamboyance and luxury and scandalous affairs

The Five Eldest Children of Charles I, by Sir Anthony van Dyck (1599–1641), 1637

Prince Charles (later Charles II) rests his hand on the mastiff's head, and is flanked to the left by his eldest sister, Princess Mary, and Prince James (later James II), and to the right by Princess Elizabeth holding his third sister, Princess Anne. This famous painting was commissioned by Charles I and twice left the Royal Collection, during the Commonwealth and under James II, before being repurchased by George III in 1765. It now hangs at Windsor Castle.

she was glad his home was fitted up so well but she warned him to put away his dogs if he wanted to have good furniture

responded with an act requiring all office-holders – most notably the Duke of York – to denounce Catholicism and take Holy Communion according to the Anglican rite.

Charles's response was to retreat behind the formality of court etiquette. Access to the monarch had been carefully controlled by the Tudors, but the process became increasingly elaborate during the seventeenth century at European courts such as Versailles, where sovereigns created ornate palaces and intricate rituals to emphasise their divine right to rule. The new royal apartments designed for Charles II at Windsor were similarly intended to impress on visitors the power and magnificence of the monarchy. Contact between the king and his important subjects was regulated and formalised as

Louise de la Kéroualle, Duchess of Portsmouth, by Philippe Vignon (1638–1701), *c.*1673

Charles II's principal mistress from 1671, Louise de la Kéroualle (1649–1734) was given her own lodgings at Windsor Castle. A back staircase led from the King's Closet to his private apartments, which gave discreet access to Louise's rooms.

those with privileged access to the monarch were filtered through the suite of increasingly splendid rooms, culminating in the private rooms for king and queen, to which only their personal and most trusted servants had access.

When Charles II first returned to England, however, the sumptuous royal apartments at Windsor that were to be created and are one of his greatest legacies could hardly have been imagined. By 1660, after years of use as nothing more than a military garrison and prison, the castle was in a dilapidated state, 'exceedingly ragged and ruinous' as the diarist John Evelyn noted sadly, its walls stripped of their paintings and the rooms of its treasures. Soon after his return, Charles set out to recover as much as possible of the dispersed contents of the royal palaces. Plate, hangings, pictures and other items were returned to the Crown daily, Evelyn observed. Seventeen cartloads of goods had been retrieved from Cromwell's widow alone. Many of the most famous paintings in Charles I's collection had been sold to collectors abroad, however, and now grace the walls of many major museums and galleries in Europe. Other Old Master paintings which had remained in England, including the series of family portraits by Sir Anthony van Dyck that now hang at Windsor, were voluntarily returned or forcibly repatriated in compliance with a series of parliamentary proclamations and other legal measures.

Charles's visits to the castle during the first decade of his reign were rare. Perhaps even more off-putting than the lack of suitable accommodation was the fact that there was no hunting to be had. Much of the parkland had been sold off during the Commonwealth, and with no one to maintain the fences, the deer had long gone. Although money was set aside to repair the palings and restock the park, it was not until 1670 that Charles was able to hunt again.

In 1668 Charles II made his cousin, Prince Rupert, Constable of Windsor Castle. Rupert had had a distinguished military career but had become increasingly interested in science, philosophy and the arts. According to Evelyn, 'he took extraordinary delight in the castle bestowing no small part of his time and Art in Beautifying and Adorning it'. Traditionally the Constable lodged in the Norman Gate, but Rupert moved into the Round Tower and put much effort into transforming it. He created a new fashion by displaying weapons on the walls of his hall in decorative patterns. Rupert was handsomely adorned and 'very singular', Evelyn wrote approvingly, although he was less impressed with the prince's bedchamber, which was

---

taking great delight in the situation and pleasant walks around it

---

'hung with tapissry, curious and effeminate Pictures'. Rupert's new decor was so much remarked upon that his sister wrote to say that she was glad his home was fitted up so well but she warned him to put away his dogs if he wanted to have good furniture.

Charles II brought the whole court to Windsor for Easter 1674, and it returned in July the same year for the summer. Entertainments included hunting in the restocked parks, plays in St George's Hall and a re-enactment of the celebrated exploits of his illegitimate son, the Duke of Monmouth, at the 1673 siege of Maastricht, staged nearby on the land between the castle and the River Thames to the north. Space was so tight at the castle that it was a struggle to accommodate all the courtiers and their

servants. The king's closest body servant, the Groom of the Stole (or Stool, to recall its original bodily function) was obliged to give up his lodging for the king's mistress, Louise de la Kéroualle, Duchess of Portsmouth. The Poor Knights were paid £200 to move out of their houses so that the queen's household had somewhere to stay, while other members of the household were forced to rent accommodation outside the castle. Those lucky enough to be allocated lodgings found them in a poor state of repair.

The dilapidated condition of the castle in 1674 seems to have convinced Charles II that changes needed to be made, and it was reported in July that he had 'given orders to make several additions and alterations to the castle and park, to make it more fit for his summer's residence every year, taking great delight in the situation and pleasant walks around it'. Responsibility for the design was given to Hugh May, who had been appointed Surveyor of Windsor Castle the previous year. May, a fervent Royalist, had been in exile with Charles II on the Continent, and with the king had observed Louis XIV's ambitious building programme at Versailles, with its awe-inspiring representation of kingship. Charles II had no intention of slavishly following the French king's model, even if he had had the funds to do so, but May's designs for Windsor Castle were deliberately designed to glorify the Stuart family and Charles II's reign.

Plans for the rebuilding were probably made during the summer of 1674 and the changes would have a lasting impact on Windsor Castle. May's design involved keeping much of the fabric of Edward III's palace as a shell, although the north wall was demolished to make way for a new block to house the king's privy, or inner, chambers. It became known as the Star Building after the

This bronze equestrian statue of Charles II by Grinling Gibbons (1648–1721) was commissioned by Tobias Rustat in 1678–9. Rustat was the King's Page of the Backstairs, who, although a servant, had amassed a fortune 'by his wonderful frugality'. According to the diarist John Evelyn, he 'did many works of charity' and spent £1,000 on the statue 'out of gratitude to His Majesty'. Unusually for the period, the statue shows Charles II as a Roman emperor with classical cropped hair.

great gilded Garter star – 12 ft (3.7 m) across – that was affixed to the outside wall. The star was also Charles II's personal emblem, adopted after a star – probably a supernova – had appeared on the day he was born.

Apart from the ornamental star and round-headed windows, May kept the exterior austerely majestic, much as it had been in Edward III's time, an effective contrast to the exuberant splendour of the new interior. As was traditional, the king and queen had their own apartments, each with a sequence of rooms through which access gradually narrowed, and each approached from the ground floor through a separate staircase. Each set of apartments consisted of a Guard

Chamber, a Presence Chamber, a Privy Chamber, a Drawing Room, a Bedchamber and a Closet. In addition, the king had a private bedroom, now known as the King's Dressing Room, and a dining room, referred to at the time as an Eating Room. This room was also accessible from the queen's apartments, while the queen, who had her own role to play in ceremonial and formal entertaining, had a gallery between her Audience Chamber and her Drawing Room. Normally a gallery was a private space, often located beyond the bedchamber, but in May's new layout Queen Catherine already had access to Elizabeth I's gallery through her bedchamber in the Henry VII Tower. The

new gallery, therefore, served as an ante-room to the Queen's Drawing Room, where she hosted an assembly known as a 'circle' where she – and sometimes the king – would mingle with courtiers. Today this room is known as the Queen's Gallery.

Any gentleman 'of quality and good fortune' or the wives and daughters of the nobility could attend court in the seventeenth century. Visitors entered through the Great Gate from the Upper Ward. Those hoping to meet the queen would head straight up the Queen's Stairs; for the king, they turned right into a hall where they were faced with a monumental triumphal arch framing the entrance to a double staircase. This led into the King's Guard Chamber, staffed, as the name suggests, by the king's bodyguard, the Yeomen of the Guard. From here a visitor would be allowed into the Presence Chamber, where the king made occasional ceremonial appearances, granting audiences to ambassadors or receiving civic delegations. Like many of the state reception rooms, the Presence Chamber was sparsely furnished, with only a 'great chayre' beneath a crimson canopy of state, two stools and a footstool with a cushion. At night, the king's 'esquires of the body' slept in the Presence Chamber under blankets and quilts.

The Presence Chamber led into the Privy Chamber, traditionally a palace's main audience chamber but rarely used as such by Charles II at Windsor. Still, it was furnished with an azure, gold and silver canopy of estate above another great chair and stools, and, as in the Presence Chamber, the walls

Known today as the Queen's Gallery, this was the Drawing Room created for Charles II's queen, Catherine of Braganza, where she would meet and mingle with courtiers. The room was remodelled in the early nineteenth century: the original panelling was replaced with silk damask wall linings and Verrio's painted ceilings with decorative plasterwork.

The King's Old State Bedchamber, by Charles Wild (1781–1835), *c*.1816

One of a number of watercolours for W.H. Pyne's *History of the Royal Residences* (1816–19) showing the appearance of the State Apartments before the extensive remodelling undertaken by Wyatville for George IV. Here the ceiling painted by Verrio can be seen still intact.

were hung with tapestries depicting the Four Seasons. Like the Presence Chamber, this room was transformed into a dormitory at night. More of the king's servants slept here: six beds (what today would be called mattresses) along with quilts, candlesticks and chamber-pots were provided for them.

From the Privy Chamber, a privileged visitor would progress to the King's Drawing Room, within the new Star Building. The name 'drawing room' abbreviates the original 'withdrawing room' when, in search of privacy, earlier monarchs would withdraw

quilts, candlesticks and chamber-pots were provided

from the relatively public audience chamber to a room with more restricted access. Once limited to those with a personal invitation from the king, the 'drawing room' had gradually become a place where the court assembled in the hope of speaking to the monarch. Eventually a 'drawing room'

The new State Apartments designed by Hugh May for Charles II were panelled in oak and incorporated elaborate wooden carvings by Grinling Gibbons, who carved these limewood garlands to frame a portrait of Queen Catherine of Braganza in the King's Dining Room. Gibbons's carvings are three-dimensional still lifes with fruit, flowers and pea pods.

referred also to a social assembly in the presence of the king or queen. Charles II held more informal receptions here, and while there was no formal canopy of state, the room did have two armchairs and ten stools as well as tables and stands carrying candelabra.

The sequence of state rooms culminated in the King's Great Bedchamber, to which only the most important guests were admitted. The bed was a symbolic piece of furniture, representing the ultimate access to the king, who held a formal *levée* in the Bedchamber in the morning. Accompanied by music, he

would be dressed by his servants while guests came and went for informal conversation with the king befitting the intimacy of the occasion. The ritual was repeated during a *coucher* in the evening before the king retired to bed.

In theory, the king slept in the next room, the Little Bedchamber, known today as the King's Dressing Room, and beyond that was his most private room, the Closet, whose walls were hung with silk and decorated with some of the king's finest small paintings. The Closet was a study, where Charles kept his most precious treasures, and only he and his trusted servant, William Chiffinch, had keys to the room.

From the Closet a door led to an even more intimate space, the king's stool room. The stool room was lined with stamped and gilded leather hangings, which were believed to be hygienic, and the seat of the close stool – grandly covering a humble chamber pot – was upholstered in velvet. The stool room was at the head of a back stair that led down to a second set of private apartments for the king. On the floor below, Charles had another bedchamber, conveniently next to the lodgings of his mistress, Louise de la Kéroualle. Beyond her rooms were those of their son, Charles Lennox, 1st Duke of Richmond. The apartments on the floor below were of equal size to the state rooms above, but the ceilings were lower and they must have been warmer and easier to heat. The king's personal body servants – pages, gentlemen-in-waiting, keepers of his wardrobe, barbers and the woman who emptied his close stool – were lodged on the ground floor, where there were also rooms for the Master of the Horse, a key member of the king's household and a role that Charles gave first to his illegitimate son the Duke of Monmouth and later to another son, the Duke of Grafton. The king's personal wardrobe was kept on the ground floor, too, and access to the back stairs was carefully controlled by Chiffinch, who was the page of the king's bedchamber and keeper of his private closet.

The queen had her own suite of rooms, culminating in a bedchamber with a dressing room, closet, private gallery and library beyond. Her servants were housed above her lodgings at the attic level, while there was a dining room for her gentlemen below her Presence Chamber. Her dogs had their own space at the foot of the stairs.

The King's Eating (or Dining) Room could be accessed from both the king and the queen's apartments. A long-established ritual of kingship, dining in public was an important part of the weekly round of royal appearances. In other palaces this was a

spectacle that usually took place in the outer chambers, where larger numbers of people could watch the king eating. At Windsor, May's design reflected Charles's desire for greater privacy and observers were limited to those privileged enough to attend the Queen's Drawing Room or to be admitted to the King's Bedchamber. A lobby was built at either end of the Eating Room to accommodate the violinists who provided music while the king was dining.

All the state rooms were lavishly decorated. The walls were panelled in oak over which expensive and colourful tapestries were hung, and the cornices were elaborately carved by a team of carvers led by Henry Phillips and Grinling Gibbons. Pictures were set into the panelling above doors and chimney-pieces, and framed with superb garlands and drops of limewood carved with fruit, fish, flowers and game.

The gilded plaster ceilings were painted by the Italian-born artist Antonio Verrio with allegories glorifying the restored monarchy and the revival of English naval power, and representing the king and queen in mythological terms. Although only three of the 19 ceilings painted by Verrio survive, his work at Windsor is considered to have been the largest and most impressive series of baroque decorative paintings ever created in the British Isles.

Verrio also painted a series of *trompe-l'oeil* scenes around the newly refashioned St George's Hall and chapel. The remodelling of the hall took place against a backdrop of tension between Charles II and Parliament, which came to a head over the largely fictitious 'Popish Plot'. This was supposedly a Jesuit plot to murder the king and raise the country in a Catholic rebellion. In this hysterical atmosphere, Parliament attempted to exclude Charles's brother, the

Above and left: Details from the painted ceiling in the King's Eating Room, now the King's Dining Room. One of only three ceiling paintings by Antonio Verrio (*c*.1639–1707) to survive at Windsor, this depicts the Banquet of the Gods, framed by a series of superb still lifes of fruit, fish and fowl decorating the coving, including a turkey (*left*) and a bright red lobster.

Catholic Duke of York, from the succession. Charles's resistance led to a struggle for authority between Crown and Parliament, and surely informed the decoration of St George's Hall and the chapel. Edward III's hall was designed for ceremonial feasting; Charles had the room decorated as a colossal throne room. Thrones were rare in the seventeenth century, when the king would usually sit on a chair dignified by the covering canopy of state. In his new hall at Windsor, Charles insisted that a dais should be built with a throne that more nearly resembled a

coronation chair. Rather than a banqueting hall, Charles envisaged a symbolic space that would be used only at the greatest state events, specifically designed to assert the majesty of kingship. Remodelled by May and painted by Verrio, Charles II's hall was a baroque masterpiece and its destruction by Wyatville in the late 1820s as part of the remodelling of the castle for George IV has been described as one of the great losses of English architecture.

The chapel was similarly decorated by Verrio with *trompe-l'oeil* scenes to reflect its

Christ Healing the Sick, by Antonio Verrio (*c*.1639–1707),
c.1678–82

Modello (sketch) in oils for the north wall of the Chapel Royal,
which served as a backdrop to the ceremony when
Charles II 'cured' people afflicted by scrofula, a disease known
as the King's Evil and believed to be cured by the touch of
a monarch.

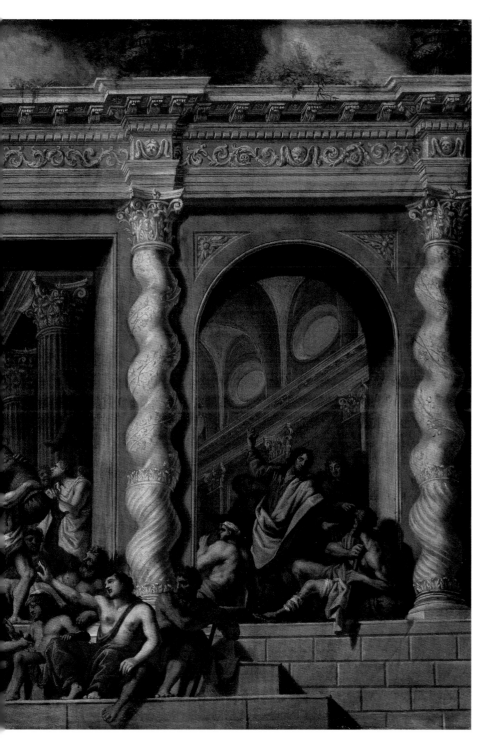

Overleaf: St George's Hall, by Charles Wild (1781–1835), *c.*1816
The interior of St George's Hall as designed by Hugh May
for Charles II and destroyed when the State Apartments were
remodelled for George IV. Wild's painting shows Verrio's
depiction of Edward III and the Order of the Garter on the
walls, and Charles II enthroned in Garter robes on the ceiling.

the less glamorous side of court life

new status as the principal royal domestic
chapel in the kingdom. The queen, as a
Catholic, attended services in her own
chapel, but Charles II had his own closet
in the newly transformed chapel next to
St George's Hall, furnished with another
chair of state as well as two high stools, a foot
stool and two cushions. However, the chapel
served another purpose, too. The glandular
disease scrofula could supposedly be cured
by the touch of a king. Charles developed the
ceremony of touching 'the King's Evil', as the
disease was known, increasing the number
of people 'touched' a year from 3,500 in the
middle years of his reign to nearly 9,000 in
1682. The new chapel was the setting for
these ceremonies in the 1680s, when the
king 'cured' the afflicted in front of Verrio's
depiction of Christ Healing the Sick, a thinly
disguised gesture underlining his belief in the
divine right of kingship.

In addition to the spectacular new royal
apartments, May tackled the less glamorous
side of court life, rebuilding lodgings for
members of the household and refashioning
Edward III's now antiquated great kitchen.
Fashions in cooking were changing rapidly,
and the great fireplaces of the medieval
kitchens no longer suited contemporary
tastes. A series of reforms early in Charles II's
reign had already drastically reduced the
number of servants below stairs, which in turn
reduced the number of those who needed
to be fed every day. Individual members of
the royal family and some senior courtiers
acquired their own kitchens and cooks.
May subdivided the great medieval kitchen
into a number of smaller kitchens for the

Left: *Michael Alphonsus Shen Fu-Tsung, 'The Chinese Convert'*, by Sir Godfrey Kneller (1646–1723), 1687

Shen had converted to Christianity and travelled to Europe with a Flemish Jesuit. He became a well-known figure at the court of James II, who commissioned his portrait shortly after Shen's arrival in England.

Right: James II, when Duke of York, with Anne Hyde, Princess Mary (later Mary II) and Princess Anne, by Sir Peter Lely (1618–80), *c.*1668–85

queen and other courtiers, and built a new 'King's kitchen' next to it. This incorporated the castle's well, which was dug deeper and equipped with a new engine to draw up water.

The remodelling of Windsor Castle cost more than £200,000 before it was finished, partially financed by the subsidy paid to Charles II by Louis XIV of France under the Secret Treaty of Dover of 1670. Charles initiated a number of building projects during his reign, but Windsor was the only one that he saw completed. Largely finished by 1684, the work was his greatest architectural achievement and Hugh May's masterpiece. Although St George's Hall and the chapel have been rebuilt, and the appearance of the royal apartments has inevitably been altered since Charles II's

reign, the layout of the state rooms and some of the surviving decoration that can be seen today still give a sense of the splendour of the Restoration court.

Charles II was proud of his new palace, but he was not able to enjoy it for very long and had no legitimate children. On his death in 1685 his brother, James II, inherited a magnificent castle that not only perfectly suited his idea of kingship but also lent itself easily to his religious beliefs. James's adherence to Catholicism was to be his downfall, however. When his second wife, Mary of Modena, bore him a son called James Edward (The Old Pretender), the birth of a Catholic heir to the throne galvanised the Protestant opposition into action. Princess Mary was James's eldest daughter by his

Side table by Andrew
Moore (1640–1706), 1699

One of the most
magnificent surviving
examples of the short-lived
seventeenth-century royal
fashion for silver furniture,
this silver side table was
made for William III.
Note the pineapple set at
the crossing point of the
stretchers. Native to South
America, the pineapple
was at the time a valuable
fruit and may have had
meanings associated with
the exotic, the dominance
of trade, or simply
hospitality and welcome.

first marriage (to a Protestant) and wife of
William of Orange, the Stadtholder of the
Netherlands and a staunch Protestant. A
group of aristocrats opposed to James invited
William and Mary to claim the throne jointly
in James's place, and in 1688 William landed
at Torbay in Devon. When it was clear that
James lacked support, he fled Whitehall and
the provisional government offered its loyalty
to William III and Mary II.

William and Mary's marriage was childless.
In 1694 Mary died from smallpox, aged only
32, and William continued to rule alone. He
had no abiding interest in Windsor Castle,
preferring Hampton Court, which he and
Mary had intended to make their main
residence as well as the principal seat of the

court, and purchasing Kensington Palace as a
place to sleep when he had to go to Whitehall
on government business.

In contrast, Mary's younger sister, Anne,
had frequently resided at Windsor with her
husband, Prince George of Denmark, since
1684. They were both keen hunters, and
happily spent their summers with the royal
buckhounds that were kennelled in Windsor
Forest. In 1686 they moved out of the castle
and leased Burford House, which had been
built by Charles II for his mistress, Nell
Gwynn, a little to the south west of the castle.
Anne gave birth to 18 children during her
marriage, only one of whom, William, Duke
of Gloucester, survived infancy.

William III disliked his sister-in-law and

her husband, and the feeling seems to have been mutual. But as Mary had died childless, Anne's son was heir presumptive and was increasingly and publicly treated so. In 1697 it was decided that the young prince should spend his summers at Windsor, where he would receive instruction from the Bishop of Salisbury. The arrangement suited Anne and her son well. Anne could hunt, while William became captain of a small army of boys from nearby Eton who drilled together and on one occasion staged a mock battle in St George's Hall. Prince William seems to have enjoyed his time at Windsor greatly, learning to ride, fight and hunt in the forest and acting in plays with his friends. When he was seven he was invested with great splendour as a Knight of the Garter, although the king was notably absent.

In 1698 Anne purchased a house immediately to the south of the castle. Known as the Garden House, this remained her favoured residence at Windsor even after she became Queen. Prince William celebrated his 11th birthday at Windsor in 1700, but complained of fatigue that night and only a few days later was dead. Distraught, Anne retired to the Garden House and barely left it for two years.

William III died in 1702 and Anne became Queen. She continued to spend most of her time at Windsor, and it was in the Henry VII Tower overlooking North Terrace that she received news of the Duke of Marlborough's famous victory over the French at Blenheim in 1704.

William III, by Sir Godfrey Kneller (1646–1723), 1690

One of a pair of portraits of William and Mary of Orange, the king is portrayed in coronation robes with the regalia resting on a table on the right.

William, Duke of Gloucester, by Sir Godfrey Kneller (1646–1723), 1699

Queen Anne's only child to survive infancy, William (1689–1700) was heir to the throne before his death aged 11 in 1700.

Opposite: Queen Anne, by Charles Jervas (*c.*1665–1714), after Sir Godfrey Kneller

The last Stuart monarch, Queen Anne loved to hunt in the Great Park at Windsor.

Anne loved racing, regularly attending the races at nearby Datchet. In 1711 she founded a new racecourse at Ascot. Hunting remained a favourite activity, and gravel-surfaced rides were laid throughout the park, allowing the queen to travel out at speed in a two-wheeled chaise to places where deer had been singled out for her to hunt.

Anne's birthday in February 1714 was celebrated with 'a great Appearance of Foreign Ministers, Nobility and Gentry, sumptuously Drest, who about Two a Clock in the Afternoon paid their compliments to her majesty; And at Night there was a ball and splendid entertainment in the castle.'

On occasions like these, the queen would occupy the State Apartments, but at other times, particularly when she was unwell, she preferred the privacy of the Garden House.

The birthday celebration of 1714 was to be Anne's last. The death of her son, William, had prompted the Act of Settlement in 1701, which ensured that a Protestant succeeded to the throne. When Anne died on 1 August 1714, the throne therefore passed to her second cousin (like Anne, a grandchild of James I), George I, Elector Prince of Hanover, whose own descendants were to have such a profound impact on Windsor Castle.

CONSERVING THE CASTLE

The Royal Collection is one of the world's greatest collections of art, and much of it is on display at Windsor Castle. Curating and conserving these extraordinary paintings, sculptures, items of furniture and other decorative pieces is the responsibility of the Royal Collection Trust, a registered charity that was founded to ensure that objects in the Royal Collection are maintained and conserved to the highest standards, and that visitors can view the Collection in the best possible condition.

All the paintings in the castle and elsewhere in the Royal Collection, from an Egyptian stela to a portrait by Lucian Freud, are cared for by the painting conservators, who carry out anything from minor *in situ* cleaning to a full structural conservation. Over the years, paintings can darken under accumulated layers of dirt and soot, while the original varnish used to protect the paint layer can also yellow with age. This often leaves the painting looking far from the artist's original intention. Conservators are able to remove these layers very carefully and return the painting to something like its original state. However, the process is only undertaken after tests to ensure that the underlying paint layers will not be harmed.

Investigative techniques and technologies such as infra-red reflectography, X-radiography and paint cross-section analysis inform more complex treatments, while 3D laser modelling may be used to create a custom support for a particularly fragile painting. In addition to the pictures hanging in the State Apartments at Windsor and elsewhere, between 50 and 100 paintings each year are displayed in exhibitions at

The Queen's Galleries or at other royal residences, while a further 40 or so are loaned to exhibitions in the UK and abroad. All must be prepared to make sure that each work is shown at its best, and the paintings conservators work closely with the curators, who are responsible for the care, display and interpretation of the paintings at Windsor Castle and a further 15 main locations across the UK where the Collection is displayed.

The Royal Collection also contains an extraordinarily wide range of three-dimensional objects, from masterpieces of baroque sculpture to Civil War munitions armour, from Sèvres porcelain to raffia work from Tuvalu, looked after by the curators and craftsmen in the decorative arts section, with the help of the Master of the Household's

'C' branch, based in purpose-built studios in Windsor. Royal Collection curators are responsible for sculpture, furniture, clocks, ceramics, silver, arms and armour, and jewellery, as well as objects produced by many cultures and peoples around the world.

One of the most interesting features of the Royal Collection is the number of objects that are not only still displayed in the historic interiors for which they were intended, but that are also used on a regular basis. The chandeliers are lit for evening receptions, the porcelain and silver-gilt services are used at state banquets. The Queen's private apartments at Windsor Castle also contain items from the Collection. As in any home, the furniture is subject to wear and tear. A team of cabinetmakers, gilders and upholsterers work on a rolling programme to keep everything in perfect condition.

Other items, particularly those with moving parts like clocks or automata, sometimes have to be repaired and new parts made, but the maintenance of the original appearance is always a priority. As with all conservation across the Royal Collection, repairs are

Left: Paper conservator releasing a drawing from an unsuitable historical mount.

Above: Conservator examining a painting in the picture conservation studio.

undertaken sympathetically and using reversible techniques.

Specialists in the conservation of historic and modern book bindings and archival material and prints and drawings are also based in studios in Windsor Castle itself. Using up-to-date but historically appropriate conservation techniques, the paper conservators stabilise and repair books with minimal interference to their original structures and can create new or facsimile bindings as required. Many of the skills used, such as edge gilding and gold finishing, have been employed since the reign of

George III, when the bindery was based at Buckingham Palace.

While the works of art at Windsor Castle are cared for by specialist conservators, the fabric of the castle itself is the responsibility of Property Services, which is part of the Privy Purse and Treasurer's Office in the Royal Household. Looking after a building as complex and historic as Windsor Castle brings unique challenges. It is a royal residence that must be maintained to the highest standards, as ready to host a state visit as a quiet weekend. It is a working environment requiring electricity, heating,

plumbing, communications and other
essentials, all of which the property services
team must be able to repair quickly. It houses
a priceless collection of works of art, much
of which requires special conditions, in
an ancient and complex fabric. It is open
to the public, so must provide a safe and
enjoyable experience for large numbers
of visitors every day. The Property Services
section not only reacts to everyday problems,
but also implements planned maintenance
programmes aimed at equipping Windsor
Castle for the challenges of the future while
at the same time conserving its exceptional
heritage and role as a working palace today.

An essential part of maintenance is the
annual 'high clean'. For two weeks in January
the castle is closed to the public and scaffolds
erected so that the State and Semi-State
Apartments can be thoroughly cleaned from
floor to ceiling. Suits of armour are cleaned,
chandeliers lowered and washed, silver
polished, carpets vacuumed and paintings
and their frames carefully dusted.

THE GREAT PARK AND HOME PARK

The forest area to the south of the River Thames at Windsor provided sport for the royal court even before the Norman Conquest. Part of the great forest had been enclosed by the time of the Domesday Survey of 1086, but it was the Normans who introduced the much-resented Forest Law to protect the 'vert' (trees and undergrowth) and the 'venison' (the animals, particularly the deer and wild boar that the Normans loved to hunt). Hunting was restricted to the nobility, and the law proscribed harsh punishments for poachers and foragers, leading to bitter complaints that wild animals were protected at the expense of the English.

In the mid-thirteenth century Henry III ordered a new park to be created south of Windsor Castle. This probably incorporated an earlier park and covered some 1,500 acres (607 hectares). It was surrounded by a park pale – a bank topped with a high timber fence and a ditch on the inside – designed to keep the deer in and poachers out. The area around the castle itself was enclosed as another deer park by Edward III in 1368, distinguished from the larger park to the south as Little Park. The two royal parks were separated by land not owned by the Crown, and although both were enlarged over the centuries, they were not connected until 1680, when Charles II bought a strip of land to enable him to lay out an avenue through which he could drive directly to the Great Park from the castle. The planting of a double avenue of elms along the Long Walk, as it became known, was completed by William III in 1696. Many of the original trees

had been replaced before the end of the nineteenth century, and an outbreak of elm disease in 1940 destroyed the remainder. The Long Walk is now planted with a mixture of planes and horse chestnuts.

Hunting remained the main attraction of the parks for many centuries. There seems to have been a Keeper of the Park from the first enclosure of the Great Park, and from the sixteenth century the Keeper was known as the Ranger of the Great Park, a role that survives to this day and is currently held by The Duke of Edinburgh. Traditionally the Keeper or Ranger was responsible for maintaining stocks of deer and preserving the environment for hunting, but the eighteenth century saw a new emphasis on idyllic rural landscapes. George III's uncle, the Duke of Cumberland, was Ranger from 1746 to 1765, and lived in the Great Park in the lodge that now bears his name. He set about transforming the southern section of the park into a picturesque landscape of glades, woodland and lakes dotted with romantic buildings. The Duke created Virginia Water, where he kept a Chinese barge, the *Mandarin*, 'as rich and gay as carving, gilding and Japanning can make

it', and built a little Chinese pavilion on an island in the middle of the lake.

His nephew inherited both the title of Duke of Cumberland and the Rangership, and continued embellishing the park but fell out with his brother, the king, who was now spending more and more time at Windsor. On the Duke's death in 1790, the Rangership fell into abeyance until George III's son took on the role, first as Prince Regent and later as George IV. George III himself developed two farms in the Great Park and designed dwellings for some of the park labourers, as well as enlarging his uncle's great lake – Virginia Water – to its present extent.

For many centuries the parks offered the royal family a retreat from the formality of court life. In the thirteenth century Henry III built a moated manor house near Virginia Water and often stayed there in preference to the castle. Later monarchs were also drawn to the houses and lodges around the parks, where they could relax with their close companions. In the 1790s Queen Charlotte was given the estates at Frogmore – between the Little Park and the Great Park – for her personal use. The house at Great Frogmore was remodelled for her in classical style, and

Left: *The Nubian Giraffe*, by Jacques-Laurent Agasse (1767–1849), 1827

George IV kept a menagerie at Sandpit Gate Lodge. It included a Nubian giraffe, the subject of this painting.

Above: Cattle from the Royal Farm grazing in Windsor Home Park.

Right: *Adelaide Cottage, Windsor Home Park*, by Caleb Robert Stanley (1795–1868), 1839

Adelaide Cottage in Windsor Home Park was a *cottage orné* built by Wyatville in 1839 as a royal retreat. Queen Victoria often visited the cottage for breakfast or tea.

the interior decorated 'in a style of elegant simplicity, in conformity with the notions of Her Majesty'. The queen and her daughters spent many of their days at Frogmore, gardening, painting, reading or entertaining. Once or twice a year, Queen Charlotte would give parties or 'fêtes', as she called them, at Frogmore. One of the grandest was the Jubilee fête held in 1809 to mark the 50th

year of George III's reign. Nearly 1,200 people were invited to an 'elegant supper', with a spectacular show staged on the lake, involving fireworks, illuminations and an elaborate water pageant celebrating the triumph of Britannia.

Mercilessly lampooned by the press, George III and Queen Charlotte's son – the Prince Regent, later George IV – secluded himself in the elaborately remodelled 'cottage' that became known as Royal Lodge in Great Park. He liked to spend his days on Virginia Water, on the banks of which he built an elaborate multicoloured pavilion. Outings from there included fishing from one boat while a band played to him from another, or visiting the menagerie behind Sandpit Gate Lodge where he kept a variety of animals, including a zebra, a leopard and a giraffe. His most lasting contribution to the Great

George III's Royal Dairy in the Home Park was rebuilt by Prince Albert. With its stained-glass windows and Minton tiles, it is a fine example of the 'art-manufactures' that the Prince was keen to promote.

Park, however, was the colossal equestrian statue erected in memory of his father, George III. Designed to be seen from the castle three miles away, the horse is so big that 12 people lunched inside it on the day it was installed in 1831.

Queen Victoria loved the parks at Windsor and in 1840, soon after her marriage, she appointed Prince Albert Ranger of Windsor Great Park, where he introduced new farming methods to increase productivity. In 1845 the royal couple founded the Royal School for children living on the estate. Prince Albert developed a model farm in the Home Park (as the Little Park had become known by the nineteenth century), with what he called 'the best cow-house in the world', and among other improvements remodelled George III's dairy, with rows of decorated basins, stained-glass windows and walls covered in Minton tiles and majolica bas-reliefs.

The Prince Consort also reorganised the kitchen gardens at Windsor, amalgamating four separate gardens into one. The new garden at Frogmore covered 60 acres (24 hectares) and included walled gardens, nurseries and enormous iron-framed greenhouses. Vegetables were planted in ordered rows around a central fountain; when it was finished, it was said to be 'the most perfect garden in Europe of its kind', supplying the royal tables 'with the finest fruits and vegetables which skill can produce'.

It was Prince Albert who moulded the Home Park into one continuous estate and diverted the public road that had previously passed through the park to allow the railway line to run along the river. In compensation for the closing of public access, a northern section of the park was thrown open to the public and has since been known as Home Park Public.

During the First World War part of the Great Park was used as an army camp; during the Second, it was ploughed up and cultivated as part of the national effort to become self-sufficient. It was not until 1979 that The Duke of Edinburgh took the decision to enclose a large section of the Great Park and revert to an enclosed deer park. Two red deer stags and 40 hinds were introduced; their descendants now number some 500 and roam freely around the enclosure.

Today the Great Park is a popular visitor attraction, its gardens, lakes, woodland and parkland able to be enjoyed by everyone, while the Home Park remains the private estate attached to Windsor Castle.

4

THE GEORGIAN CASTLE

Queen Charlotte, by Benjamin West (1738–1820), 1779

Thirteen of the queen's 15 children can be seen behind her. The Prince of Wales and Prince Frederick stand on the left, wearing the 'Windsor Uniform' designed by their father, George III, with the ribbon and star of the Garter. In the background is a view of the south front of Windsor Castle. The long, narrow building in front of the castle is Queen's Lodge, which was built to house the Royal Family in the late 1770s because the castle had fallen into disrepair during previous reigns. The lodge was later demolished by George IV.

The first Hanoverian kings had little interest in Windsor Castle; indeed, it received so little attention during the reigns of George I and George II that the years after Queen Anne's death are often referred to as the castle's 'long sleep'. Although the royal apartments were reserved for occasional royal use, the rest of the lodgings were used as grace-and-favour apartments, mostly occupied by the 'antique dowagers' recalled by Charles Knight, the son of a Windsor bookseller, who played in the Quadrangle as a boy. Throughout the eighteenth century the castle precincts were open to the public, as were the State Apartments, and in spite of its increasingly dilapidated air Windsor was a popular and picturesque destination for early tourists. Daniel Defoe (1660–1731) described it as 'the most beautiful, and most pleasantly situated castle, and royal palace, in the whole isle of Britain'.

George I and George II may not have cared

---

the most beautiful, and most pleasantly situated castle, and royal palace, in the whole isle of Britain

---

for Windsor, but Frederick, Prince of Wales, and eldest son of George II, was a frequent visitor. He enjoyed hunting in the Little Park and was well aware of the 'rare and excellent pictures at Windsor'. Frederick, like his son and grandson, was a keen collector of art but he died in 1751, and on George II's death in 1760 it was Frederick's son, George III, who became King at the age of 22.

The new king was described by Horace Walpole as having 'a great propensity to the arts' and a particular interest in building. Unlike his predecessors, he was passionately patriotic and a great respecter of Britain's history and traditions, embodied in Windsor Castle. George III hunted frequently in the Great Park and attended the Ascot races, but it was not until 1776 that he moved his family to Windsor. By then Queen Charlotte was 32 and already had seven sons and four daughters, aged between 12 and less than one. Rather than using rooms in the castle, the royal family occupied Queen Anne's Garden House. After a large programme of work, partly carried out to the king's designs, the house was renamed Queen's Lodge; it provided a favourite residence throughout the 1780s and 1790s.

A daily routine was soon established. The royal family attended prayers in the Royal

the place I love best in the world

Chapel next to St George's Hall at 8am and then breakfasted back at the Queen's Lodge. The king would ride and attend to business matters in the morning, while the queen wrote letters, was read aloud to, or played the harpsichord. Meanwhile, the elder princesses had lessons between 9am and noon. Dinner was served between 3pm and 4pm, and in the evening social events would start around 7pm. In summer the royal family would often gather at the castle to walk on the terrace before returning to the Lodge for tea, music and cards around 9pm. Many of the evening gatherings were quite informal – or as informal as they could be with a band of musicians playing in the next room. In 1777 George III gave the queen her own private band, which played on the castle terrace every night when the royal family was in residence, and in the Queen's Lodge. One visitor described the royal family sitting 'round a large table, on which are books, work, pencils, and paper … In the next room is the band of music, who play from eight o clock till ten. The king generally directs them what pieces of music to play, chiefly Handel's'. Cards and backgammon were popular evening activities too.

The years at the Queen's Lodge were clearly happy ones. George III enjoyed playing the role of country squire and described Windsor

George III, by Thomas Gainsborough (1738–1820), 1780–1
The king wears the 'Windsor Uniform' coat of dark blue with gold facings and red collar and cuffs, which he designed for formal wear at the castle and which is still worn by male members of the Royal Family at Windsor.

Above: *The Quadrangle looking West*, by Paul Sandby (1731–1809), *c.*1765

Sandby's watercolour shows the original height of the Round Tower and position of the equestrian statue of Charles II before the changes made by Wyatville under George III's successor, George IV. During George III's reign, the Quadrangle was open to the public, and although beggars were supposed to be refused entry by the sentries, clearly some slipped through.

Right: Mantel clock, by Matthew Boulton (1728–1809), 1770–1

Commissioned by George III, the clock was made partly to his own design.

as 'the place I love best in the world'. He liked a morning walk and regularly visited the different parts of the park, genially greeting those who lived and worked there. Nicknamed 'Farmer George' for his interest in agriculture, he reclaimed large areas of Windsor Great Park to lay out two farms, each managed according to a different pattern of cultivation. The king took a close personal interest in the farms and submitted various articles on farming methods to the Board of Agriculture written under the *nom de plume* of his shepherd, Ralph Robinson. He also developed a dairy farm in the Home Park, which supplied butter, milk and cheese for the royal table.

George III was interested in building as well as farming, and soon turned his attention to the castle itself. He was keen to restore and refurbish the State Apartments, and to enhance the traditions and historical

No beggars or disorderly persons, women in red cloaks or pattens are to be allowed to walk upon the Terrace at any time

significance of Windsor Castle and of the Order of the Garter. The King's Closet was enlarged by knocking through into an ante-room, and in 1786 the King's Audience Chamber was modernised. George III envisaged it as a Garter Throne Room where new Knights could be installed. The room was given a new marble chimney-piece and the walls were hung with Garter-blue velvet trimmed with floral needlework borders. The impressive canopy over the throne was embroidered with matching needlework. In the other state rooms the dark wainscoting was replaced with a brighter damask wall covering, and more elaborate fireplaces were installed.

In 1788 the King fell ill. His illness is now thought to have been porphyria, but the symptoms of confusion, delusion and mania were frightening, and after a scene in the queen's apartments in the Queen's Lodge on 5 November that year, it was decided that the king should be moved to Kew, where he could be treated in greater privacy than at Windsor. He recovered the following year, but the queen refused to be alone with him again, and they led increasingly separate private lives, although they continued to appear together on formal occasions.

George III was happy to return to Windsor after his recovery, and to resume the family routine. Evening gatherings on the North Terrace were once again a regular part of royal life and very popular with visitors, who liked to see the king and queen 'unattended by pomp or state', and sometimes even to exchange a few words. There were few

Previous page: Windsor Castle from the North, by Antonio Canaletto (1697–1768), 1747

The exterior of the walls of the Little Park can be seen to the left, while the River Thames is to the right.

restrictions about who could enter. The sentries were certainly ordered to 'keep every thing quiet about their respective posts' and in 1781 the castle's governor issued further instructions:

No beggars or disorderly persons are on any account to be allowed to pass their posts and no coaches are to be allowed to stand in any of the Gate ways … The sentries at the King's Gate and Governor's Door are not to permit any servants or boys to gallop about the court. No higglers to be allowed to bring any meat, fish or greens to sell in the Court Yard of the palace, nor are any articles to be cried out for sale in any part of the palace. No beggars or disorderly persons, women in red cloaks or pattens are to be allowed to walk upon the Terrace at any time.

With the king back at Windsor, the castle came to life again. A party to celebrate the king's recovery was held on 1 May 1789, with dancing in the 'Great Room' (the King's Guard Chamber and now the Grand Reception Room). The royal table was laid with a new silver-gilt dining service and decorated with 'temples in barley sugar, four feet high, and other devices introducing the motto and emblematic of peace and joy'.

The later changes introduced by the king at Windsor may have been made in reaction to political events. The crisis in America and the eventual loss of the American colonies had made him unpopular for a time in the 1770s, but the tide of public opinion swung back in his favour after the French Revolution overthrew the traditional structures of society across the Channel in the 1780s and 1790s. The king found himself increasingly attuned to the traditions and the continuity of English institutions. The shift in attitude was reflected in the popularity of the Gothic Revival, an architectural movement that was

The Queen's Drawing Room, by Charles Wild (1781–1835), c.1816

Wild's watercolour shows the room as it was when used by Queen Charlotte for entertaining. It is hung with tapestries and paintings purchased by George III, while the set of painted seat furniture was part of the late eighteenth-century refurbishment of the State Apartments. The ceiling painted by Verrio for Charles II was replaced by Waytville in the 1830s.

seen as native and patriotic, distinguishing monarchical, Christian England from revolutionary, anti-clerical France. As a young man George III had received lessons from the classical architect Sir William Chambers, and his early interventions at Windsor were in the classical style. But the king later embraced the Gothic style, which he considered perfectly suited to Windsor Castle; in 1796 he appointed James Wyatt, a leading proponent of the movement, to oversee the improvements.

Wyatt set about re-Gothicising the castle, inside and out. He added towers and doorways, and a new Grand Stair rising to a landing outside the King's Drawing Room. There were other changes, too, but generally the improvements put in place by George III and Wyatt respected the ancient rooms. Wherever possible, Gibbons's carvings were preserved and sometimes copied, while Verrio's painted ceilings and the great murals in St George's Hall and the Royal Chapel were repaired and repainted where necessary.

When the refurbishment of the State Apartments was finished in February 1805, George III insisted on a 'housewarming' party to show off the work that had been done. Government ministers and 290 other 'persons of distinction' were invited to the castle to hear a performance of Handel's *Esther* in the Queen's Audience Chamber, followed by dancing in the Queen's Gallery, which became known for a time as the Queen's Ballroom. The Queen's Band played while supper was served in the King's Guard Chamber, and the plate on the royal table was again silver gilt. The guests ate off silver, and the tables were spread with damask tablecloths bearing royal arms made from yarn 'spun by the Royal hands of the lovely Princesses'.

That event was itself surpassed in magnificence by the feast that followed the first Garter installation ceremony for more than 30 years. A spectacular banquet was held on St George's Day 1805 in St George's Hall, with subsidiary eating areas throughout the castle and dancing as usual in the King's Guard Chamber. This was to be the last Garter installation service before the twentieth century, and the last Garter feast of all.

There were parties for children too, particularly after the Prince of Wales's daughter, Charlotte, was born in 1796. On Christmas Eve 1800, other high-ranking children were invited to 'a German entertainment' at the Queen's Lodge:

There was a yew-tree in a tub, placed in the middle of the room; from the branches hung sweetmeats, almonds and raisings, apples, and toys of various kinds; and the whole was illuminated with little wax candles. The children walked round … then each child had a share of the sweetmeats; and a toy, and went home highly gratified.

The redecoration programme of the State Apartments carried out 'under direction of His Majesty' had involved the transfer of a number of fine paintings to Windsor and the delivery of new furniture, including a splendid new bed for the Queen's Bedchamber. George III added considerably to the royal collection, in particular to the collection of Old Master drawings now kept in the Royal Library at Windsor Castle. His most important acquisition was the purchase in 1762 of Joseph Smith's collection of art. Smith had been British Consul in Venice, and during the course of his career had collected a large group of works by Venetian artists, including more than 40 by Canaletto, most of which are still hanging on the walls at Windsor. An inventory of paintings at the castle taken in 1813 listed 357 works, 213 of which hung in the State Apartments and 83 in the king's private apartments.

Opposite: Embroidered canopy of the state bed attributed to Robert Campbell (active 1754–93), *c.*1778

The tester bed was supplied to Queen Charlotte in 1778 for the Queen's State Bedchamber. Made of carved giltwood, it was hung with beautifully embroidered satin curtains. Much of the richly flowered and botanically accurate embroidery was stitched at Mrs Phoebe Wright's 'Royal School of embroidering females', an institution actively supported by Queen Charlotte.

the Coldest House, rooms, & Passages, that ever existed

With the refurbishment of the State Apartments on the way to completion, the king decided to move into the castle himself, directing his architect, James Wyatt, to 'alter and decorate a wing' as a royal residence. His health continued to be unstable, but in November 1804 the royal family moved from the Queen's Lodge into the castle. The king took the 'Lower Apartments' in the north range overlooking the North Terrace, below the old state apartments and once Charles II's private suite of rooms. Queen Charlotte had rooms in the east range and south-east tower. The rooms were elegantly decorated and furnished in the latest style but the queen had mixed feelings about the move: 'I have changed from a very Comfortable & warm habitation, to the Coldest House, rooms, & Passages, that ever existed', she wrote to a friend. In spite of a further £4,500 spent on furnishing the apartments, they remained cold and draughty, and three years later another letter from the queen described how she and her daughters sat huddled in their pelisses 'to prevent our being frozen'. She and her princesses often spent their days instead at Frogmore House, which the king had bought for her in the early 1790s.

The Tribuna of the Uffizi
(detail), by Johan Joseph
Zoffany (1733–1810),
1772–7

Commissioned by
Queen Charlotte, the
painting shows a group
of identifiable English
collectors admiring the
treasures of the Medici
collection in Florence while
on a Grand Tour of Europe.
The tour was considered
an important part of a
gentleman's education
at the time. In the detail,
two young visitors draw a
Greek statue of Cupid and
Psyche while a group of
men discuss a Madonna by
Raphael. Zoffany himself
holds up the painting.

In 1810 George III succumbed once more to the manic episodes that had afflicted him in 1788. It was said that he had 'quite Lost himself, and Recollects People that have been Long Dead', and in February 1811 the Prince of Wales was declared Regent. The king remained at Windsor, visited occasionally by his family and ministers, but was increasingly left alone with his doctors. He was confined to three rooms, with furniture 'of the most homely description', and the bed in which he died on 29 January 1820 was described as 'hardly larger or more luxurious than the commonest kind of officer's camp bed'.

George IV, as the Prince Regent now became, was of course long familiar with Windsor. On his 18th birthday he had been given a complete set of apartments in the east range, 'fitted up in an elegant & proper manner'. When he was 21 the apartments were extended, his allowance was increased and he was given his own London residence, Carlton House. One of the monarchy's greatest patrons of the arts, he added a seaside residence in Brighton, but when he requested a country house in 1785, George III, dismayed by his son's extravagance, put his foot down: 'as to a country house, I have none for him … his apartment at Windsor shall always be kept ready to receive him'.

The Prince Regent did not share his parents' willingness to mingle with the public, and he spent little time in his apartments in the castle, especially after his marriage to Caroline of Brunswick broke down in acrimony. The death of their daughter, Princess Charlotte, in 1817 was not only a huge personal blow to the Prince Regent but also triggered a rather unseemly rush among his ageing brothers, who unexpectedly found themselves in line for the throne and had to make respectable marriages in the hope of producing an heir.

After 1811 the Prince Regent returned to Windsor, but preferred to reside in the Great Park, living in what is now called Royal Lodge, where he could be more private. However, once George III had died the castle was effectively abandoned by other members of the royal family, and the terraces were closed to the public except on Sundays. In 1823 the new king moved into Queen Charlotte's apartments in the east range (which had been allocated to him in the 1780s and 1790s) and stayed for two months, during which time he seems to have made plans for an extensive renovation of the Upper Ward. The State Apartments in the north range had been designed for the etiquette of a different era and were unsuitable for the requirements of a new age, while the private apartments were, in George IV's view, inconvenient and outdated.

George was advised in his plans by his close friend Sir Charles Long. Capable, cultivated and well connected, Long drew

up an architectural competition with eight questions for prospective architects to consider, and the king invited four architects to submit designs. The competition was won by Jeffry Wyatt, nephew of George III's architect James Wyatt, whose designs offered an elegant solution to George IV's requirements, creating a grand but convenient residence for the sovereign in the east and south ranges, remodelling the State Apartments and providing more accommodation for the royal household with updated service areas. Wyatt proposed a fundamental alteration.

According to his scheme, the east and south ranges would be transformed into manageable residences, linked at principal floor level by a gallery 560 ft (270.7 m) long, the 'Grand Corridor'. The sovereign would live entirely on this floor, while the service rooms would be on the ground floor and an upper storey would be added to provide accommodation for servants and household members. A grand new gateway would be built on the south side of the Quadrangle, the east range would be remodelled to provide a magnificent suite of reception rooms and the parkland to the south and east of the castle, which had been open to the public, would be closed off. Furthermore, the Round Tower was to be raised to improve the way the castle appeared from a distance and a special chamber was to be created, a 'Waterloo Gallery', to house the portraits that the king had commissioned from Sir Thomas Lawrence to mark the coalition of military commanders, statesmen and diplomats whose efforts had defeated Napoleon and secured a lasting peace after years of war.

George IV laid the first stone on the site of the new George IV Gate on his 62nd birthday in 1824. On the same day Jeffry Wyatt changed his name to Wyatville, after requesting the king's permission to do so: 'veal or mutton', said George in response, 'call yourself what you like'.

The first phase of the work lasted four years. It soon became clear that the castle was in worse condition than had been realised, with cracked walls, rotten timbers and 'very bad' foundations throughout. Inevitably the costs soared, but the work continued and by December 1828 George IV was able to move into the newly completed east and south ranges. Wyatville handed the king the keys to the castle in a crimson bag, and was knighted in reward for his services.

The new apartments were sumptuously

decorated and furnished. George IV was strongly francophile. He spoke fluent French and in the course of his life brought together the finest collection of decorative art ever assembled outside France. He bought large quantities of fashionable French furniture for the royal palaces, much of it acquired as a result of the confiscation of royal and aristocratic property during the French Revolution, and as a result the Royal Collection contains outstanding examples of the work of the best eighteenth-century French cabinetmakers.

George IV's tastes as a collector were wide. In addition to furniture, he purchased Old Master and contemporary paintings, sculpture, and plate, arms and armour and porcelain. One of his favourite activities was to discuss and make decisions about the decoration and furnishings of the new interiors created for him by Wyatville. Many items of furniture and fittings now at Windsor came from his first London residence, Carlton House, which was demolished in 1827. Not everyone admired the excess of gilding, but George IV's new rooms at Windsor are now considered to be the finest and most complete example in existence of the late Georgian taste for French furniture and decoration.

Once the king was established in his new apartments, work moved on to the second stage of the project, remodelling and redecorating the state rooms. The seventeenth-century State Apartments had been designed for the baroque court, whose rituals were very different from those of the early nineteenth century. George IV's priorities were not those of Charles II. He needed a throne room, with large rooms for the musical entertainments, balls and banquets that were the staple of nineteenth-century court life. The old King's Presence

Previous page: The Crimson Drawing Room was intended as the principal reception room of George IV's new private apartments at Windsor. The king took a personal interest in all aspects of the decoration and furnishings of the room, which reflects his taste for gilding, rich colours and ornate design.

ready to fall in patches on the slightest disturbance

Chamber and King's Audience Chamber were united to form a single larger throne room, while the King's Guard Chamber, used so often for dancing in George III's time, was transformed into a proper ballroom, now known as the Grand Reception Room. All but three of Verrio's painted ceilings were lost in the renovations; the ceilings were found to be so dilapidated that they could not be saved. The plaster was said to be 'ready to fall in patches on the slightest disturbance'. The same situation was found in St George's Hall, where Verrio's murals, regarded by many as a baroque masterpiece, were destroyed. The royal chapel was demolished and the hall itself extended and redesigned in what was thought of as a more appropriately 'medieval' style. The author of an official guide to the castle commented on the hall when it reopened: 'although we miss the Cupids and the Muses, and gay and gaudy paintings of the Italian artist, still it may be supposed that the nature of the present decorations, and their pure simplicity of style, are more accordant with the grandeur of the hall, and harmonize more with the character of its patron saint'.

Two of the more dramatic improvements planned by George IV were still unfinished at the time of his death. The first was the raising of the Round Tower. Wyatville underpinned the walls and relined them with brick before doubling their height and capping them with a corbelled and battlemented parapet. On top of this was a Flag Tower, and a flagstaff, fixed more than 50 ft (15.2 m) higher than it had been, and installed in February 1831, thus creating the instantly

Pietra dura cabinet, by
Martin-Eloy Lignereux
(1752–1809), 1803

Commissioned in Paris for
George IV when Prince of
Wales, this is one of a pair
of ebony-veneered oak
cabinets decorated with
pietra dura panels depicting
birds and vases of flowers,
originally supplied for
Carlton House and moved
to the king's bedroom at
Windsor Castle in 1827–9.

recognisable silhouette of Windsor Castle.
Uncompromisingly medieval at first glance,
this famous view of the castle is a creation of
the early nineteenth century.

Another of George IV's long-standing
ambitions had been to create a chamber
celebrating the end of the Napoleonic Wars.
He had commissioned Sir Thomas Lawrence
to paint a series of portraits of those involved
not just in winning the war but also in
negotiating a lasting peace, and he wanted an
appropriate room to display them. The vision

was George IV's but the Waterloo Chamber
was not built until the reign of his brother
William IV, who succeeded him in 1830.

After a lifetime of over-indulgence, George IV
did not age well. As a young man he had
been genial and charming, but he suffered
from dropsy in later life and took pain-killing
drugs that, together with his huge appetite
for food and drink, left him swollen and
immensely fat. Preferring to spend his days
secluded from the public gaze, the king
often stayed at Royal Lodge, his extravagantly

The Angle of the Grand Corridor, by Joseph Nash (1809–78), 1846

The Grand Corridor was George IV's most extensive and novel addition to the castle. Designed by Wyatville to link the royal and visitors' apartments to the State Apartments, the Corridor provided a place for the king to display some of the choicest paintings, furniture and *objets d'art* in his collection. Some of the furniture, including stools by A.W.N. Pugin that can be seen on the left, were specifically designed in the Gothic style for the Grand Corridor, which has remained little changed to this day.

remodelled *cottage orné* in the Great Park, from where he could doze and fish on Virginia Water, lunch in the Chinese Fishing Pavilion or visit his menagerie at Sandpit Gate. Queen Victoria remembered him as kindly when she visited him at Royal Lodge as a girl: 'Give me your little paw', he said as he helped her up into his carriage and took her for a drive around the park.

As George IV's health deteriorated, he spent more time in his private apartments in the castle, which he liked to keep overheated, to the discomfort of his guests. He often spent much of the day in bed and, as his eyesight failed, an attractive actress (Eliza Chester) was engaged to read to him from the works of his favourite novelists and playwrights. But he continued to entertain friends and to eat and drink in gargantuan quantities, in spite of his doctors' warnings. The Duke of Wellington visited in April 1830 and reported that for breakfast alone the king had eaten two pigeons and three beef-steaks from a pie while drinking 'three parts of a bottle of Mozelle, a glass of dry champagne, two glasses of port [and] a glass of brandy!' All this on top of regular doses of laudanum.

Three months later George IV died at Windsor. 'My dear boy!' he exclaimed as he grasped his doctor's hand in the final moments, 'This is death!' His funeral took place in St George's Chapel, the burial place of his daughter, Princess Charlotte, and he was laid to rest with his family in the Royal Vault created for George III.

He was succeeded by his brother, William IV, a bluff retired naval officer who shared few of his brother's tastes and whose interest in the arts was minimal. Shown one of the masterpieces in George IV's collection, he did his best to appreciate it: 'Aye, it seems pretty', he commented. 'I dare say it is. My

for breakfast alone the king had eaten two pigeons and three beef-steaks from a pie while drinking 'three parts of a bottle of Mozelle, a glass of dry champagne, two glasses of port [and] a glass of brandy!'

brother was fond of this sort of nick-nackery.' However, he continued George IV's restoration of Windsor, giving Wyatville permission to begin the next stage of work on the State Apartments and to begin filling in Horn Court to create the Waterloo Chamber. By 1832 the Grand Stair built by James Wyatt for George III had been replaced by a new Grand Staircase, and the Waterloo Chamber, the Ballroom (now the Grand Reception Room), St George's Hall and the new Guard Chamber were all complete.

William IV and Queen Adelaide brought a new tone to the monarchy. They moved into Windsor Castle two weeks after the funeral of George IV, marking the occasion with a public dinner given to the poor, fireworks and a grand ball held in Windsor's Town Hall. The East Terrace was reopened to the public. The new king and queen were hospitable and entertained on a grand scale. There were dinners and house parties, usually including William's large but illegitimate family. He had ten children by his long-term mistress, the actress Mrs Jordan, who was put aside when the death of Princess Charlotte caused a constitutional crisis and made it imperative for George IV's brothers to contract respectable marriages. Queen Adelaide had no surviving children of her

Above: Miniatures of Queen Adelaide (1792–1849) and William IV (1765–1837), by William Essex (1784–1869), 1846

Left: The Waterloo Chamber was created by Wyatville from what was once Edward III's Horn Court. The Chamber was designed to display the series of portraits commissioned by George IV to celebrate the end of the Napoleonic Wars, while the ceiling evokes a man-o'-war ship from the time of Nelson.

own, but kindheartedly welcomed the king's children to Windsor. Charles Greville, invited to dinner in 1831, could only marvel at the change at Windsor Castle: 'no longer George IV, capricious, luxurious and misanthropic, liking nothing but the society of listeners and flatterers, but a plain, vulgar, hospitable gentleman, opening his doors to the whole world with a numerous family (all illegitimate)'.

William's lack of legitimate children meant that his heir was his niece, Victoria, daughter of his brother, the Duke of Kent. Normally a jovial host, William intensely disliked Victoria's mother, the widowed Duchess of Kent, and at his birthday banquet in St George's Hall on 21 August 1836 he caused a public sensation by launching into a tirade against her in front of a hundred guests. He hoped that when he died royal authority would pass directly to 'that Young Lady', he

My brother was fond of this sort of nick-nackery

said, referring to Princess Victoria, and not to the Duchess, 'the person now near me, who is surrounded by evil advisers and is herself incompetent to act with propriety in the station to which she would be placed'.

The king's wish was to be granted. Princess Victoria celebrated her 18th birthday on 24 May 1837, just four weeks before William IV died at Windsor. In many ways her reign marked the heyday of Windsor Castle, but in character, decoration and detail it remains George IV's creation, and his taste informs in large part the castle that visitors see today.

VISITING THE CASTLE

Henry II entertained William II of Scotland at Windsor Castle in the twelfth century, and the castle has provided a suitably magnificent setting to impress important visitors ever since. Conveniently close to London, there was room in the Great Hall for feasting, and elsewhere for lodging, while the Little and Great Parks offered ample opportunities to entertain guests with ever-popular hunting. Although visits from heads of state were by no means unknown before the nineteenth century, it was then that state visits became more common and assumed a set pattern.

Royalty from around the world came to Windsor during Queen Victoria's reign: King Louis Philippe of France – and his usurper, Emperor Napoleon III – Frederick Augustus, King of Saxony, the Tsar of Russia,

Emperor Pedro II of Brazil and the Emir of Afghanistan were all welcomed by the Queen, who came down to the State Entrance to greet a fellow monarch but stood at the top of the Staircase and waited for other ranks of royalty to come up to her. On these occasions the stairs were lined with an impressive display of the Yeomen of the Guard or soldiers of the Household Cavalry in full dress uniform. 'Are they real?', the son of the Emir of Afghanistan asked when he visited with his father in 1895, and stroked one to check that he wasn't a waxwork. The Queen then took her royal visitor to the Garter Throne Room, where she introduced her family. Until Prince Albert's death, a state ball would be held on the first evening of a royal visit, with a grand dinner in St George's Hall and dancing

This page: A procession of horses and carriages from the Royal Mews forms part of an official welcome for state visits.

Opposite, left: St George's Hall prepared for a state banquet.

Opposite, right: Reception of the Emperor and Empress of the French at Windsor Castle, 16 April 1855, by George Housman Thomas (1824–68), 1855

in the Waterloo Chamber, but Victoria never danced again after 1861, and the state ball was replaced by musical entertainment.

Today Windsor Castle continues to provide a spectacular backdrop for state visits and other official visits by foreign heads of state. The visiting head of state is welcomed in the Home Park Public to the accompaniment of military bands and an artillery salute. Horses and carriages from the Royal Mews then form a procession with The Queen and other members of the Royal Family, which takes the visiting dignitaries through the decorated streets of the town to the Long Walk and into the Upper Ward through the George IV Gate. A royal dais is set up in the Quadrangle and the royal party watches as successive ranks of the Household Cavalry, the Mounted Band

Below: Plates from the priceless collection of dining services are still used for state banquets. From the top: dessert plate from the silver-gilt Grand Service acquired by George IV when Prince Regent; a plate from the Minton Dessert Service made in 1877 and decorated with Queen Victoria's VR cipher; and one of a set of eighteenth-century Tournai porcelain plates decorated with birds and butterflies.

Above: Place settings for a state luncheon in the Waterloo Chamber.

of the Household Division and the King's Troop, Royal Horse Artillery file past in a spectacular display of pageantry and military precision that echoes the military displays that were already a key part of medieval diplomacy when Edward III laid out the outlines of the Upper Ward.

State visits are planned several months in advance, and involve all branches of the Royal Household. On the first night of the visit The Queen hosts a state banquet in St George's Hall, where a table long enough to seat 160 people is polished to a high shine and precisely laid with a glitter of gold, silver and glass.

Not all visitors to Windsor Castle come at the invitation of the monarch. The reduction in dynastic feuding in the sixteenth century made travel

Claret being decanted using traditional wine decanters and muslin cloths.

safer, and the curious were keen to see the castle. In the absence of the monarch, those with leisure and means could apply to the housekeeper and be shown around the State Apartments. Paul Hentzner accompanied a Silesian nobleman to Windsor in 1598 and admired 'two bathing-rooms, ceiled and wainscoted with looking-glass' as well as a chamber containing five royal beds, 'all of them eleven feet square and covered with quilts shining with gold and silver' and Queen Elizabeth's bed, which he said was not as long or as large. As if this were not enough, they were shown other curiosities in the same room, including a bird of paradise, a cushion 'most curiously wrought by Queen Elizabeth's own hands' and a unicorn horn valued at more than £10,000. Baron Waldstein, visiting a couple of years later, was similarly impressed by the curiosities and the beds: 'I never saw bigger in my life'.

By the time of the Restoration, 'all persons or gentlemen of quality and fortune' and 'all wives and daughters of the nobility, and their women that attend them … and all other ladies of good rank and quality' were able to get as far as the Presence Chamber and have a look around. If they were lucky, they could also see the king receiving a public deputation, or eating a public dinner. The intrepid Celia Fiennes, riding into Windsor in 1698, was able to get a much closer look at the rooms. She seems to have been able to poke around wherever she wanted, and even inspected a 'a little place with a seate of Easement of Marble with sluces of water to wash all down' in the little Garden House to the south of the castle, used by the future Queen Anne as her Windsor residence.

In 1666 Samuel Pepys and his wife were taken on a tour of St George's Chapel, the Upper Ward and the royal lodgings, which impressed them greatly. Pepys later wrote in his diary: 'It is the most romantique castle that is in the world'.

The State Apartments continued to be open to the public on application to the housekeeper, and guidebooks were regularly published to help the curious make their way round the castle. Joseph Pote, an Eton bookseller, was given a royal licence to publish *History and Antiquities of Windsor Castle* in 1749. The success of this led to him publishing a few years later 'a lesser work on the same subject, and extracted from the above History, in French, and English, for the Use and Accommodation of Strangers, and other Persons who visit this Royal Castle'. Called *Les Delices de Windsore*, it sold for 2s and included a plan 'Shewing Alphabetically at one View the several Appartments in the Royal Palace as shewn to ye Publicke'.

After George III and his family took up regular residence at Windsor, the castle became increasingly popular as a tourist destination. Almost every part of the castle outdoors was open to the polite public, who could join the royal family on their daily promenade on the terraces. Most days, the only other strollers would be townspeople and other castle residents, but the Sunday promenade soon developed into a special occasion that drew grand visitors from London and the surrounding countryside.

George IV did not share his parents' informal attitude to meeting the public, and he had the terraces closed for privacy. But the State Apartments were reopened to the public by Queen Victoria in the 1840s, and during the second half of the nineteenth century around 60,000 visitors passed through the rooms each year. The two major wars in the twentieth century interrupted public access to the castle once more, but access to the State Apartments has gradually

increased since the 1950s. After the fire of 1992 and subsequent restoration, the Semi-State Apartments were opened to the public for the first time, and visitor numbers rose to an unprecedented level. A new admission centre was built in the Lord Chamberlain's Lower Stores to the south of the Lower Ward, and today more than a million people from around the world visit Windsor Castle each year. An active Learning section now exists

too, to make the castle and its collections
more accessible to the public through a
variety of different events, from lectures
and creative courses to storytelling sessions,
activity trails for children and family festivals.

Queen Victoria on Open Sunday, published in Joseph Nash's
(1809–78), *Views of the Interior and Exterior of Windsor Castle*,
1848

The reopening of the State Apartments to the public and the
expansion of the railways in the second half of the nineteenth
century brought increasing numbers of visitors to the castle.

INTERIOR DECORATION

During the Middle Ages furniture tended to be sparse and mostly portable: stools and benches, screens and trestle tables that could be quickly put together and then dismantled at night so that members of the household could sleep in the hall. Important chambers might be splendidly decorated with painted and gilded stone and woodwork, but they remained largely empty spaces until the arrival of the court, at which point the rooms were transformed with elaborately draped beds, chairs of state and displays of gold and silver plate and other fine objects. Painted hangings and tapestries gave warmth and richness to the rooms.

When Charles II came to remodel the State Apartments at Windsor, the rooms were decorated to dazzle and impress visitors with a splendid setting for the monarchy. New furniture was ordered, including great chairs of state set under gorgeously coloured canopies, stools, armchairs –

Queen Catherine had two armchairs covered in flowered velvet – tables, looking glasses, torchères to hold candelabra, some spectacular silver furniture, and a great bed of state hung with crimson damask and gold silk and silver fringing.

By the eighteenth century, tastes had changed. When George III and Queen Charlotte moved in to their new apartments at the castle in 1804, they were decorated in a restrained classical style. The panelled walls and coved ceilings were painted in two or three pale tones and ornament limited to graceful friezes or the occasional vertical panel modelled with bands of plaster foliage.

Restraint was to vanish under George IV, who reacted not only against George III's politics but also against his father's taste for the cool order of the Enlightenment. As Prince of Wales and later Prince Regent, he filled first Carlton House and then the Royal Pavilion at Brighton with a gorgeous

George IV commissioned many pieces of furniture to be made up to agreed designs. This sketch by Thomas Talbot Bury (1811–77) for a 'Table in the Corinthan Room, Carlton House' was made by Thomas Parker (active 1808–30). The table was part of the group of furniture and furnishings supplied between 1827 and 1829 to George IV by the partnership of Morel & Seddon for the Library (now the Green Drawing Room) at Windsor Castle.

Above: Design for the east elevation of the Great Drawing Room (the Crimson Drawing Room), Windsor Castle, by Morel & Seddon, *c.1826*

One of the 'miniature designs' produced by Morel & Seddon for the approval of George IV. The designs show the intended detail of curtains and upholstery and the disposition of furniture.

Opposite, far left: The magnificent curtains in the Crimson Drawing Room and the adjoining rooms, with their complex fringing and tassels (*passementerie*), were made after the fire of 1992 and are closely based on Morel & Seddon's original designs.

assemblage of art and colour. George IV revelled in luxury and comfort. He liked glitter and gilding, rich colours and ornate design, extravagance and exuberance. He also had an excellent eye for art, and a flair for display.

As a result he took an intense and personal interest in the interior decoration and furnishings of the new rooms created for him at Windsor by Jeffry Wyatville. Wyatville had little interest in furnishings, but incorporated into his designs marble chimney-pieces, carved and gilded doors, wall panels and frames, pier glasses, chandeliers, stained glass and parquet floors sent from Carlton House.

To help furnish his new apartments at Windsor, George IV appointed Nicholas Morel, who ran a fashionable business supplying high-quality furniture and furnishings. Morel employed a team of artists to make detailed drawings with measurements of the furniture and anything else that might be used from Carlton House, which enabled him to create 'miniature designs' to show the king how the finished rooms would look.

Morel went into partnership with the large and well-established furniture-making firm of Seddon's in order to fulfil the enormous contract. Together Morel and Seddon were responsible for supplying all the new furniture for Windsor Castle, copying existing pieces to make pairs or sets and altering and restoring older pieces in the royal collection as well as George IV's new purchases. They provided gilded frames, silk for the walls, curtains and upholstery in addition to the furniture. The cost of their contract between 1825 and 1830 came to more than £270,000. They worked closely with the team that George IV had assembled over the years to create the rich interiors that appealed to him so much: celebrated decorators Frederick and John Crace, the plasterer Francesco Bernasconi, carvers and upholsterers and some new talent, including the 15-year-old boy-genius A.W.N. Pugin, who was employed to design Gothic furniture and fittings for the new Dining Room and other Gothic interiors. F.-H.-G. Jacob-Desmalter, a distinguished designer of seat furniture and other carved giltwood, was brought on board too, while

Morel himself probably concentrated on the upholstery, especially the curtain designs with their sophisticated dressing, the tassels and rosettes and fringing and other decorative elements collectively known as *passementerie*.

George IV adored poring over the designs produced by Morel & Seddon and would annotate them by hand, abandoning any interest in affairs of state in favour of the minutiae of the decoration. For the new rooms at Windsor he settled on two different styles. The entrance, processional spaces such as the Grand Corridor, principal staircases and eating rooms were to be furnished in a Gothic style, while the drawing rooms and royal

apartments would be fitted out in a version of the king's favourite classical French manner.

A number of pieces of Gobelins tapestry 'peculiarly applicable to the furnishing of some Rooms in Windsor Castle' were acquired from France at a total cost of nearly £2,500, together with three elaborately inlaid Boulle armoires, and some ebony chairs worth £480. At the end of May 1825 the king 'thought it right' to make one of his largest-ever purchases of French furniture and works of art at a sale in London, arguing that it was 'quite appropriate for Windsor Castle, and worth double what it cost'.

The king's taste for all things French was well known, but the design of the interiors came at a time when there was public unrest at the government's proposals to relax trade restrictions with France. Morel & Seddon assured the *Morning Herald* that 'the strictest orders were given by His Majesty … that if any pattern or article whatever fixed on by His Majesty could not

be manufactured in this country, that we were immediately to mention it and something else would be substituted, as everything in the castle was to be of British manufacture'.

There were inevitably alterations and redecorations to George IV's splendid rooms over succeeding generations. The devastating fire of 1992 led to some calls to rebuild in a modern style but the fortunate survival of most of George IV's collection of furniture meant that a decision was taken instead to restore many of the principal rooms as far as possible to their Georgian appearance. George IV had created at Windsor a spectacularly decorated and furnished palace, and the restoration of its sumptuous fabrics, glowing colours and glittering gilt and glass was a testament not only to the superlative craftsmanship of the early nineteenth and late twentieth centuries, but also to the taste of a king who remains one of the greatest of royal collectors.

5

THE VICTORIAN CASTLE

As the British Empire expanded and communications improved, visitors from all over the world came to Windsor Castle. George IV's remodelled State Apartments provided a stupendous backdrop for a series of glittering state visits which showed the castle at its best, the tables decked with gold plate and the drawing rooms thronged with royalty. At the same time, Windsor Castle was a home for Queen Victoria's nine children and the setting for many happy family occasions. But the death of the Prince Consort in 1861 overshadowed the last 40 years of Victoria's reign and cast a melancholy pall over the castle where he had died.

Having celebrated her 18th birthday barely a month before William IV died at Windsor, Queen Victoria came to the throne without the need for another Regency and at last escaped her mother's controlling regime at Kensington Palace. Moving smartly into Buckingham Palace, the young Queen revelled in her new life in London. She embarked on a hectic round of theatre, opera, musical entertainments and balls, beside which Windsor Castle could at first offer little competition.

Victoria had been fond of both her uncles, George IV and William IV, and when it

Scene at Windsor Castle, The Whole of the Royal Family in 1850 (after Edward Wells), by Abraham Le Blond (1819–94) and Robert Le Blond (1816–63), 1850

Windsor Castle was the setting for many happy family occasions during the earlier years of Queen Victoria's reign. This charming scene shows the Queen and Prince Albert at a window in the castle, looking down on six of their children playing below.

I passed such a very pleasant time here; the pleasantest summer I ever passed in my life

was proposed that her mother's brother, Leopold, King of the Belgians, should visit her at Windsor Castle in August 1837, she was dubious about the idea: 'Windsor requires thorough cleaning, and I must say I could not think of going in sooner after the poor King's death. Windsor always appears very melancholy to me, and there are so many sad associations with it.' As it turned out, the visit was a great success and by the time the Queen moved on to Brighton she was 'very sorry indeed to go! I passed such a very pleasant time here; the pleasantest summer I ever passed in my life'. Her initial doubts were forgotten. Rejecting the rooms where both George IV and William IV had died, Victoria had chosen to move into apartments in the south-east corner of the Quadrangle, in a tower now known as the Queen's Tower. Here she had a sitting room and dressing room with a 'lovely view', as well as a 'sweet little Bedroom'.

a good breakfast ... of a mutton chop and mashed potatoes &c

The summer had been spent riding in the parks or walking, or if the weather was bad, playing shuttlecock (an early form of badminton) with her ladies-in-waiting in the Grand Corridor or the breakfast room. At the outset of her reign, the new Queen relied heavily for advice on the Prime Minister, Lord Melbourne, and he came regularly to Windsor over the summer. Victoria often received him in the Audience Room in her private apartments, describing it afterwards as the 'nice little blue Closet where I saw Lord Melbourne'.

It was in the same room that the young Queen proposed to her first cousin, Prince Albert of Saxe-Coburg-Gotha, during his visit to Windsor Castle with his brother, Ernest, in 1839. Albert accepted, and they were married at St James's Palace in London on 10 February 1840, returning to Windsor for a short honeymoon.

Prince Albert had a wide range of interests and a love of the outdoors that meant the royal couple spent more time at Windsor after their marriage, especially as their family grew. Although Victoria and Albert visited for the Ascot races in June, Windsor was primarily a winter residence, where they celebrated Christmas and New Year, and often their wedding anniversary in February.

Life at the castle soon fell into a contented routine. Prince Albert liked to work early in the morning, in what he called 'the golden hour', and was up by 7am. Breakfast was served at 9am. This was a substantial meal and usually shared with any family members who might be around. In September 1838

Above: Design for the Queen's Audience Room, by John Thomas (1813–62), 1861

Queen Victoria met her ministers in the Audience Room in Windsor Castle and it was here that she proposed marriage to Prince Albert. In 1850 the room was redecorated as a celebration of the British monarchy and of the Queen and Prince Albert's places in the royal lineage.

Right: Queen Victoria's sketch of her dachshund, Daphne, 1849

Windsor Castle in Modern Times, by Sir Edwin Landseer
(1803–73), 1841–3

A scene of domesticity at the castle, with Queen Victoria,
Prince Albert, the Princess Royal and the 'dear dogs' Eos,
Dandy Dinmont, Islay and Cairnach, together with some dead game.

The scene is set in the White Drawing Room at Windsor,
decorated with the Morel & Seddon furniture commissioned
by George IV, and with a view of the East Terrace in the
background, where Queen Victoria's mother, the Duchess of
Kent, can be seen enjoying a circuit in a bath chair.

The White Drawing Room, from Joseph Nash's *Views of the Interior and Exterior of Windsor Castle,* 1848

For the first years of their marriage, Queen Victoira and Prince Albert regarded Windsor Castle as the family home. Nash's picture shows them at breakfast in the White Drawing Room.

the Queen, who enjoyed her food, had 'a good breakfast … of a mutton chop and mashed potatoes &c', while other breakfasts might include fish, eggs, bacon, sausages, roast meats and the occasional vegetable as well as toast and breads – and porridge after Victoria discovered the pleasures of a Scottish breakfast. Members of the household had a separate breakfast room where breakfast was served punctually at 9.30am, and included any leftovers from the royal dining room.

When Victoria and Albert were first married, breakfast was usually followed by a walk, regardless of the weather. Afterwards, they would return to the castle and deal with any business, or perhaps draw or etch together before luncheon at 2pm. If the Prime Minister had an audience with the Queen, that would take place after lunch, and between 5pm and 6pm there was often an opportunity for the Queen and Prince Albert to drive out together. Dinner was at

8pm if dining with guests or the household, and the company broke up around 11pm. Once or twice a week the couple dined in private, or with their children as they grew older. In June 1857 the Queen, Prince Albert and their eldest daughter, Princess Victoria, ate dinner alone together. Between the three of them they had the choice of two soups,

a little fir tree … covered with bonbons, gilt walnuts, and little colour tapers

one a clear chicken soup and the other with poached eggs, as well as sole gratin and fried whitings, roast beef and capon with asparagus, vol-au-vents with béchamel sauce and grilled eggs, an apricot flan and waffles 'mit crème'. Typically the meal also included cold cooked chicken on the sideboard, and fruit for dessert.

As Victoria and Albert's family grew, Windsor Castle became a family home once more, although of their nine children only Alfred – known in the family as Affie, and later made Duke of Edinburgh – was born at Windsor, on 6 August 1844. When small, the children occupied nurseries on the second floor of Victoria Tower and were cared for by nursery maids, overseen by a governess. They remained in the nursery until they were six, when they entered the schoolroom and came under the care and instruction of a range of governesses, Swiss, German and French as well as British.

The whole family often spoke German to each other, and many of their traditions were German ones. At Christmas, presents were exchanged on 24 December. After lunch the family inspected the presents, which were set out around a Christmas tree in three separate rooms: one for the Queen's mother, the Duchess of Kent, and the children; one for the Queen; and one for Prince Albert. There

The Queen's Christmas Tree at Windsor Castle, by James Roberts (c.1800–67), 1850

The Queen and Prince Albert followed many German traditions, including the setting out of gifts around separate Christmas trees. The watercolour shows the Queen's tree on a table surrounded with presents, including paintings and a bracelet designed by Prince Albert.

A Performance of Macbeth in the Rubens Room, Windsor Castle, 4 February 1853, by Louis Haghe (1806–85), 1853

Queen Victoria enjoyed the theatre and opera, and performances were put on at the castle for the whole family and their guests to enjoy. This watercolour shows the Queen, Prince Albert and the Duchess of Kent watching Lady Macbeth (Mrs Charles Kean) in the sleepwalking scene of Shakespeare's play *Macbeth* (Act V, Scene ii). The royal children are seated in a row in front of their parents on the dais.

were presents, too, for the household, which assembled in the evening in the Oak Room (at the south-east corner of the Quadrangle) to admire another Christmas tree – 'a little fir tree, in the German fashion, covered with bonbons, gilt walnuts, and little colour tapers' – and to receive their own gifts, their names written on a slip of paper by the Queen. Christmas dinner included a baron of beef (the one served in 1860 weighed 360 lb and required four men turning a spit for ten hours to roast it) and 'Wild Boar's Heads & Brawn, all ornamented with holly & Evergreens, & 3 Xmas trees which were lit at dessert', as one of the Queen's ladies recorded.

On 1 January the Queen's band played a chorale on the East Terrace under the window of the private apartments to wake the royal family in the morning, and later small gifts and New Year's cards were exchanged. This was followed by a visit to the Riding School, where food and blankets were distributed to the poor of Windsor.

Victoria and Albert were both musical, and many composers and soloists were invited to Windsor Castle to perform in private for the royal family. Victoria enjoyed the theatre and opera too, and went regularly when in London. Between 1848 and 1857 Albert arranged for the actor and theatre manager Charles Kean to direct and perform a series of theatrical performances at the castle over the winter. The King's Drawing Room became a temporary theatre, with a stage rigged up in the bay window and the

I never saw anything more amusing

adjoining rooms used as dressing rooms. Kean and his wife Ellen put on a wide range of plays, from Shakespeare to farces. A farce called *Twice Killed* went down very well with the royal party: it 'kept us in fits of laughter', wrote the Queen. 'I never saw anything more amusing.' Evening performances were followed by refreshments in the Garter Throne Room. Sometimes the royal children performed in the evenings instead, acting in charades or putting on a *tableau vivant*, which involved dressing up in costume and reciting a verse, or holding a static pose to represent a painting or a scene from a drama. When they were older they graduated to performing plays, often in French and specially commissioned from their French governess, or giving recitals.

Early in their marriage, the Queen and Prince Albert took a great deal of pleasure in sorting through and arranging (or rearranging) the castle's remarkable historic collections of paintings, arms and armour, prints, drawings, books, miniatures and, later in the 1850s, photographs. Together they rearranged the hang of the pictures at

Queen Victoria was a keen artist and often sketched her children. Her drawing of Victoria, Albert, Alfred and Alice was made in July 1846.

Windsor Castle, concentrating paintings by particular artists in one room. Pictures by Rubens were hung together in the King's Drawing Room, Van Dycks in the Queen's Gallery and sixteenth-century portraits, including a group of Holbeins, in the Queen's Drawing Room. Many of their private evenings were spent sorting through the nearly 500 historical paintings that were brought from Hampton Court to Windsor in 1843–4, or the huge collection of prints that would eventually be housed in the Print Room created by Albert in the old private apartments on the floor below the north-western end of the State Apartments.

Victoria's reign saw rapid development in many fields, perhaps none more so than in transport. Encouraged by Albert, the Queen travelled by train for the first time on 13 June 1842. The journey involved driving from Windsor to Slough, where the Great Western Railway provided a special waiting room for the royal party. A brand new steam engine was used to pull the elaborately upholstered royal carriage with three other carriages and three luggage trucks the 18 miles (29 km) to Paddington Station. Victoria declared afterwards that she was 'quite charmed by it', but although travelling by train became a regular way for the royal family to move around the country, the Queen remained adamant that the royal train's speed should be limited to 40mph, and 30mph at night.

In 1849 two new railway stations opened in Windsor: the Central station opposite the west wall of the Lower Ward, at the end of a new branch line from Slough for the Great Western Railway, and the Riverside station to the north, at the end of a new line for the South Western Railway. These stations enabled increasing numbers to visit Windsor Castle, which became a popular day trip from London. Improvements in the

*a brilliant, successful &
pleasant dream, the recollection
of which will always be firmly
fixed in my mind*

railways were matched by those in shipping, and as the British Empire continued to expand, Windsor Castle became the focus of global interests. Visitors came to Windsor from around the world. The Shah of Persia, the Emir of Afghanistan, the Emperor and Empress of Brazil, the King of Italy, Kaiser Wilhelm II, all visited the Queen. The Kaiser was Queen Victoria's grandson, one of an increasing number of European crowned heads with a close (if difficult) relationship to the Queen. Representatives from far-flung colonies came to pay their respects, together with ambassadors and emissaries of foreign governments. The Grand Vestibule in consequence soon became cluttered with displays of exotic gifts.

For state or private visits to Windsor, the Upper Ward could easily accommodate the large entourages that royal visitors brought with them and the State Apartments offered a spectacular setting for the ceremonial. For a state visit, a banquet was always held in St George's Hall, providing an opportunity to deck the table with George IV's dazzling gold plate and with flowers from the hothouses at Frogmore.

Alexander, son of Tsar Nicholas I of Russia, visited in 1839 and following his visit, the Tsar sent the Queen the magnificent malachite urn that stands in the Grand Reception Room as a gesture of thanks. The King of Prussia and other royal guests stayed for the christening of the Prince of Wales in 1842, while 1844 was a busy year with Frederick

Augustus, King of Saxony, the Tsar of Russia himself and King Louis Philippe of France all visiting at different times. Like all royal guests, Louis Philippe was treated to a magnificent banquet in St George's Hall, with a choice of turtle soup, turbot, larded venison fillets, calf's head, truffled capons, lamb's feet, vol-au-vents, grouse, stuffed lettuces, cardoons, champagne jelly, pineapple jelly and poached apricots with a pudding rice border.

By 1855 Louis Philippe had been overthrown and Britain was allied with a new French ruler, the Emperor Napoleon III. He and his wife, the Empress Eugénie, were invited to Windsor in 1855 with the specific aim of dissuading the Emperor from his plan to lead the allied armies during the Crimean War.

Much effort went into planning the visit, which involved considerable redecoration of the old state apartments. The Queen's Gallery, known then as the 'Vandyke Room', was lavishly refurbished. The walls were hung with crimson silk, the furniture upholstered in green silk and a red, gold and maroon carpet was laid on the floor. Empire-style curtains were made from green Lyons silk with green velvet for the borders and pelmets. In the King's Bedchamber, a late eighteenth-century bed acquired by George IV was installed and reupholstered in the rich green and purple silk incorporating the imperial eagle and the emperor and empress's monograms that it retains today.

The Emperor and Empress arrived at Windsor on 16 April 1855 and were greeted in the Quadrangle by Victoria and Albert, who escorted them up the Grand Staircase for presentations in the Garter Throne Room and Grand Reception Room. The imperial couple were then accompanied to their rooms before a banquet in St George's Hall. For the next two days the Emperor and Empress were entertained with music and

Left: It was during Queen Victoria's reign that state visits assumed a set pattern of protocol and pageantry. George IV's bed was reupholstered in the Napoleonic colours of green and purple and moved to the King's Bedchamber for the State Visit of Napoleon III and Empress Eugénie in 1855.

Previous page: The Quadrangle during the State Visit of Nicholas I and the King of Saxony in 1844, by Joseph Nash (1809–78), published in 1848.

The Prince Consort's Model Farm, Windsor and *The Cattle Yard of H.R.H. The Prince Consort's Flemish Farm, Windsor,* published in the *Illustrated London News,* 8 January 1859

The model farms set up by Prince Albert at Windsor incorporated the latest agricultural thinking, and the magnificent farm buildings were designed to demonstrate his belief that high art could be successfully wedded to industry and mechanical skills.

HIS ROYAL HIGHNESS THE PRINCE CONSORT'S MODEL FARM, WINDSOR.
(AFTER ORIGINAL SKETCHES BY OUR OWN ARTIST.)

THE CATTLE YARD OF HIS ROYAL HIGHNESS THE PRINCE CONSORT'S FLEMISH FARM, WINDSOR.

dancing in the Waterloo Chamber – tactfully renamed the 'Music Room' – and huge dinners in St George's Hall. It was all a great success. After musing on the strangeness of George III's granddaughter dancing with the nephew of his greatest enemy, Victoria recorded in her Journal that the whole visit had been 'a brilliant, successful & pleasant dream, the recollection of which will always be firmly fixed in my mind'.

Other less formal occasions were held at the castle in those years. Small dances were held in the Crimson Drawing Room, while larger events such as concerts and operas took place in the Waterloo Chamber, which was also used for the annual Waterloo banquet held in June, a tradition established after the Duke of Wellington's death. The most regular formal event was an invitation to 'dine and sleep', a tradition first established by Queen Victoria that continues to this day. On these occasions, ministers, foreign ambassadors and others prominent in public life were invited to Windsor Castle for dinner with the Queen and Prince Albert and members of the household, followed by conversation and occasionally cards in one of the drawing rooms. It was an honour not without some discomfort. As the courtier and diarist Charles Greville noted in 1838, most of the guests and household spent their time standing around, or leaning surreptitiously against a wall to take the strain off their feet. There was, he said,

no room in which the guests assemble, sit, lounge, and talk as they please and when they please; there is a billiard table, but in such a remote corner of the castle that it might as well be in the town of Windsor; and there is a library well-stocked with books, but hardly accessible, imperfectly warmed and only tenanted by the librarian.

Prince Albert had a notably wide range of interests, from art and architecture to sanitation and agriculture. Not only was he responsible for reorganising the Royal Library in the Elizabethan gallery, but he also embarked on the task of arranging and cataloguing the great collection of miniature paintings inherited by the Queen.

The Prince Consort was just as interested in what went on outside the castle. He was appointed Ranger of the Great Park in 1840, and found an outlet for his enthusiasm for improving art, industry and the condition of the labouring classes in the parks beyond the castle. One of his most notable architectural contributions at Windsor was to oversee the restoration of the Lower Ward, which had not been part of Wyatville's great reconstruction scheme. In contrast to the Upper and Middle Wards, the Lower Ward had remained a hotchpotch of buildings, many dating back centuries and in a ruinous condition. The architect Anthony Salvin was employed by the Prince Consort to restore a consistently medieval character to this area. This involved pulling down some buildings and obtrusive gables, replacing Georgian sash windows with smaller, narrower 'medieval' ones, repairing

part of the curtain wall and constructing a new guardhouse. The end result was tidier and more consistently Gothic in style, although inevitably not everyone was pleased: 'I have no opinion of P. Albert's taste', sniffed one critic.

Among all his projects Albert also found time to take an interest in the major sewerage and drainage project that was required to deal with the castle's ancient sewage system. In 1848 the Lord Chamberlain had to point out that nothing had been done to improve the connection between the new main drains and the water closets and sinks. 'The noxious effluvia which escapes from the old drains and numerous Cess Pools still remaining, is frequently so exceedingly offensive as to render many parts of the castle nearly uninhabitable', he complained, 'and scarcely any portion can be said to be entirely free from effects of imperfect drainage.' Accordingly, new sewers were constructed which could be flushed from tanks daily, and modern drains made of vitreous glazed earthenware were laid below the ground floor while the Quadrangle was 're-formed, drained, gravelled, and paved so as to preserve an even, clean, and dry surface'. Within the castle, 139 water closets were added or replaced, incorporating the latest invention of a flushing siphon trap. New advances in technology also led to the installation of a heating system, whereby 17 new boilers heated water at 21–27 degrees and warmed the air through iron pipes.

It was not just the castle's ancient drainage

a noise calling, hollowing, shouting accompanied by the sounds of rushing water & crashing timbers &c

system that was a cause for concern. Its vulnerability to fire was proved on the evening of 19 March 1853, when a defective chimney flue caused a fire in the Prince of Wales's Tower, just above the State Dining Room. The damage was considerable, as a large part of the Dining Room ceiling collapsed under the weight of the water and the rest was left in a perilous state. The servants' bedrooms on the floors above were gutted, but the prompt salvage of furniture and carpets meant that nothing was lost from the principal rooms. The commotion was observed by the Queen, who congregated with her ladies in the Green Drawing Room. Whenever the intervening doors opened they 'could see a scene of great excitement, – the Dining room open, – light flaring, – crowds of servants hurrying along removing the furniture, with wonderful rapidity. Such a noise calling, hollowing, shouting accompanied by the sounds of rushing water & crashing timbers &c.' The fire was eventually extinguished by 4am, and the ceiling in the Dining Room later replaced with a modified version of Wyatville's original design.

The happy routine at Windsor Castle came to an abrupt end in 1861. Prince Albert's health, never strong, deteriorated after catching a chill; he died on 14 December in the Blue Room at Windsor Castle, probably from a combination of Crohn's Disease and pneumonia rather than the typhoid that is often cited as the cause of death. Queen Victoria was with him at the end: 'I stood up, kissed his dear heavenly forehead and called out in a bitter and agonising cry "oh! My dear Darling" and then dropped on my knees in mute, distracted despair', she wrote in her Journal.

The loss of her beloved husband was one from which the Queen would never fully recover. Grief-stricken, she retreated to the privacy of Osborne House on

The State Dining Room, by Joseph Nash (1809–78), 1848

The ceiling in the State Dining Room collapsed during a fire in 1853 and was replaced in a less elaborate style. The 1992 fire consumed the entire room, which has been restored to Wyatville's Gothic design, seen here.

19 December. Prince Albert's funeral took place on 23 December 1861 in St George's Chapel, where his body lay in the Royal Vault until the following December when it was moved to the mausoleum that the Queen had commissioned at Frogmore. The royal household was plunged into mourning. For two years the liveried palace servants wore black instead of scarlet. After two years the Queen's daughters and ladies of the household were permitted to wear grey, white or lilac – the colours of half-mourning – but the Queen herself remained dressed in the black of deep mourning for the rest of her life.

When Victoria returned to Windsor on 6 March 1862 she went straight to the Blue Room where Albert had died. The novel by Sir Walter Scott that the Prince had been reading was still by his bed. The Queen had it placed in the Royal Library with an inscription marking the page he had reached, but otherwise ordered that nothing was to be changed until she gave further instructions. These were never forthcoming, and for the next 40 years the room was kept exactly as it had been in December 1861. The glass from which Prince Albert had taken his last dose of medicine remained on the bedside table. Fresh clothes were laid out every morning and hot water placed on the washstand. Each evening when she was at Windsor, the Queen knelt to pray in 'the sacred Blue Room', where she returned often throughout the rest of her life for solace.

A remarkable shrine to Prince Albert's memory was created on the site of Henry III's original chapel in the Lower Ward. The shell of the chapel built by Henry VII was retained, but the interior of what is now called the Albert Memorial Chapel was replaced by a design by Sir George Gilbert Scott (architect of the Albert Memorial in Kensington Gardens, London), with inlaid marble panels on the walls, vaults encrusted with gold mosaic and new stained-glass windows. However, Albert himself was buried in the newly erected Royal Mausoleum in the grounds of Frogmore.

Above: The Blue Room, Windsor Castle, by William Corden the Younger (1819–1900), *c*.1864

The Prince Consort's bedroom, where he died on 14 December 1861, was lovingly preserved by Queen Victoria as a private memorial to him.

Opposite: Frogmore: Interior of the Royal Mausoleum, by Henry William Brewer (1836–1903), 1869

The mausoleum was commissioned by Queen Victoria in 1863 for the Prince Consort and herself and is the finest expression of Prince Albert's personal taste. The Queen's white marble effigy was commissioned at the same time as the Prince Consort's and kept in store until her death in 1901.

*Queen Victoria and Princess
Beatrice in the Queen's Sitting
Room, Windsor Castle,* by
Mary Steen, 1895

Princess Beatrice was
companion, confidante and
personal secretary to Queen
Victoria. The photograph
was taken after breakfast on
21 May 1895. Mary Steen
was a Danish photographer
recommended by the
Princess of Wales, who was
herself Danish.

Prince Albert's death changed Windsor
completely. The Queen continued to spend
time at the castle, but was so rarely seen in
public that she began to be referred to as the
'Widow of Windsor'. Life went on and the
rituals of court continued to be observed, but
the sense of melancholy was palpable. After
Victoria's initial grief at Albert's death had
subsided, the 'dine and sleeps' were resumed,
but in a much more sombre atmosphere. If
anything these occasions were even more
uncomfortable than before. The Queen was
notoriously impervious to cold and liked to
have the windows open, which left her guests
to shiver in draughty and barely heated

rooms. Guests gathered before dinner in the
Grand Corridor between 8.30 and 8.45pm
to await the Queen's arrival from her private
rooms in the Queen's Tower, a tradition that
puzzled Consuelo Vanderbilt, the American-
born Duchess of Marlborough. Why, she
wondered, did they have to wait in a corridor
when there were any number of rooms in
the castle in which they could have waited in
comfort?

If the guests were lucky, there was music
in the Drawing Rooms after dinner, but
otherwise the ladies were invited one at a
time to sit next to the Queen for a stilted
conversation, which they could never initiate
themselves, while the other guests stood or
walked around the room. It must have been a
relief when the Queen retired. Although the
ladies had to go to bed at the same time, the
gentlemen could if they wished smoke in the
billiards room. Victoria disliked gaslight, and
until the introduction of electric light at the
very end of her reign the castle was largely
lit by beeswax candles in the chandeliers,
extinguished at the end of the evening. The
billiard room was on the ground floor at the
far west end of the north wing, so far away
from the bedrooms that stories were told
of guests who could not find their way back
again in the dark and had to spend the night
on a sofa in the state rooms.

Victoria's daughters became her closest
companions and she relied upon them to
such an extent that the younger princesses
were only allowed to marry on condition that
they continued to live nearby. The Queen had
hoped that her youngest daughter, Beatrice,
would not marry at all, and although Beatrice
was permitted to marry Prince Henry of
Battenberg, she continued to live with her
mother after their marriage in 1885 and
the Battenberg children were brought up
at Windsor Castle. A new generation in the

royal nurseries, they were able to enjoy some of the more spectacular events that took place in the later years of Victoria's reign. 'Buffalo Bill' gave a command performance to the Queen and others on the East Lawn at Windsor in June 1892. Victoria much admired the displays of horsemanship and marksmanship in the show, which involved cowboys cracking whips, a 'Red Indian' war dance, Mexicans, Argentinians and Cossacks. An equally interesting spectacle arrived at the castle the following month. George Sanger's travelling circus troupe paraded in the Quadrangle before a performance that also took place on the East Lawn. The Queen was impressed by the sheer size of the troupe, noting in her Journal:

100 horses, 50 ponies, 7 elephants, 5 lions, 3 camels, a cage of tigers, leopards & puma, 1 of Kangaroos, 1 of monkeys, 3 Llamas, an Indian bull, 30 male riders, 20 female, 9 coloured men in carriages &

elephants, 10 carriages with men representing different nationalities, 10 Thoroughbred horses & ponies, led by grooms, & Bands.

Concerts began to be held again in the castle after 1876, when the Queen's spirits were lifted by listening to selections from Mendelssohn, Gounod, Verdi and Rossini in St George's Hall: 'It was such a real elevating pleasure to hear anything of the sort again, for the first time since '61', she wrote. Her second son, Affie, was passionate about music and a key figure in the establishment of the Royal College of Music. He and his amateur orchestra performed with the Queen's private band in the Waterloo Chamber in November 1880 before an audience that included the Queen, the household and many of the servants. Invited to perform one of Gilbert and Sullivan's comic operas, *The Gondoliers*, at the castle in 1891, the D'Oyly Carte Opera Company constructed a temporary stage and

'Buffalo Bill' at Windsor, by John Charlton (1849–1917), 1892

The horsemen of Buffalo Bill's Wild West Show, performed for Queen Victoria at Windsor on 25 June 1892.

seating in the Waterloo Chamber, where the acoustics were particularly good. The Queen enjoyed the performance so much that the Lord Chamberlain's department bought the staging and the Waterloo Chamber became the normal venue for occasional operas, operettas and concerts, another tradition that has continued to this day. More intimate recitals, such as that by Franz Liszt, who played his own compositions for the Queen in 1886, tended to take place in the White Drawing Room.

The last few years of Victoria's reign were punctuated by three great celebrations, for her Golden and Diamond Jubilees, in 1887 and 1897, and to mark her 80th birthday in 1899. Victoria commemorated her Golden Jubilee by commissioning the Danish artist Laurits Tuxen to paint *The Family of Queen Victoria in 1887*. Set in the Green Drawing Room, the painting shows the Queen surrounded by 54 of her relatives and emphasises Victoria's sense of family and her links to royal dynasties across Europe. Some poetic licence was taken, as not everyone was in the room at exactly the same time, but the family was almost all at Windsor and argued greatly about their positions in the painting. At the Queen's request a clock that usually stood on the mantelpiece in the Green Drawing Room was replaced in the picture by a bust of Prince Albert.

In 1883 the Queen had tripped downstairs at Windsor and injured one of her knees. It left her lame and often in pain. Exhausted by the Golden Jubilee celebrations, she was glad to be pushed again in the 'rolling chair' that had been used for her confinements. The chair was used more and more frequently in her last decade, and in 1893 a lift upholstered

Five of Queen Victoria's grandchildren photographed in the grounds of Windsor Castle in July 1890

Seated in the donkey carriage are Princess Victoria Eugénie of Battenberg (in frilly bonnet), Prince Alexander of Battenberg and Princess Margaret of Connaught. Princess Patricia of Connaught sits on the driver's seat and Prince Arthur of Connaught rides the donkey and holds the dog lead. The groom, Beaumont, stands by the donkey's head.

Queen Victoria's youngest daughter, Princess Beatrice, was only allowed to marry Prince Henry of Battenberg if she continued to live with her mother, so the Battenberg children grew up in the Queen's household, spending their childhood at Windsor Castle, Balmoral, and Osborne House on the Isle of Wight.

The Family of Queen Victoria, by Laurits Tuxen (1853–1927), 1887
Queen Victoria had links to royal dynasties across Europe. This painting by Tuxen, commissioned to commemorate her Golden Jubilee, shows the Queen surrounded by 54 of her relatives and descendants in the Green Drawing Room.

in crimson and gold was installed in the private apartments to save her having to use the stairs.

By the time of Victoria's 80th birthday in 1899 she was feeling her age, and the celebrations were a quieter family affair at Windsor Castle. There was a family dinner attended by all her surviving children except for her eldest, Vicky, and was followed by a performance of part of Wagner's *Lohengrin* in the Waterloo Chamber, which 'enchanted' the Queen.

Queen Victoria left Windsor for the last time on 18 December 1900. As had become her habit since Albert's death, she spent

Christmas at Osborne House, and wrote in her Journal on 1 January 1901: 'Another year begun, & I am feeling so weak and unwell that I enter upon it sadly.' She suffered a stroke on 16 January and died on 22 January 1901, surrounded by her children and grandchildren. Her funeral was held in St George's Chapel on 2 February 1901 and she was buried in the mausoleum at Frogmore, next to Prince Albert, whose death she had mourned for so long.

RUNNING THE CASTLE

During the Middle Ages, responsibility for running Windsor Castle in the absence of the monarch was given to the Constable. It was a prestigious appointment, often made as a mark of favour to those closest to the sovereign, although in 1660 the outgoing Constable of the Commonwealth Castle handed it over to his successor with the rueful conclusion that 'the office of Constable of Windsor Castle is of very great antiquity, honour, power, and pleasure, but of very little profit'. Over the years, the role of Constable became conflated with that of Governor, and today it is the Constable and Governor who represents The Queen at Windsor Castle during her absence.

The day-to-day running of the castle is overseen by the castle superintendent. Often a retired military officer, the superintendent is responsible for the delivery of all routine operations and the busy programme of events and activities within the castle, as well as ensuring the maintenance of appropriately royal standards. The castle is staffed by members of the Royal Household, an institution that dates back to at least the twelfth century, when royal lodgings were divided into two key spaces, the Hall and the Chamber. The Hall was where the king appeared in public. It was a place of ceremonial and feasting, but also where the bulk of those who made up the household ate and slept. To discuss important or intimate matters, the king retreated to an inner Chamber, often on a higher level, to which only the privileged had access. The Chamber was run by the chamberlain, the Hall by the steward, roles that developed into great offices of state, the Lord Chamberlain and the Lord Steward.

Then, as now, the household moved with the monarch and the court was less a place than the people who supported the sovereign. As a general rule, the Lord Chamberlain dealt with ceremonial and political events in the household while the Lord Steward was responsible for the practical running of day-to-day life 'below stairs'. At first, kings and queens were served by nobles in the most intimate aspects of life: rising, dressing, washing, using the garderobe, waiting at table. These were honourable and prestigious positions, and titles such as lady-in-waiting still reflect their original roles in personal service. However, the business of attending to the personal

Opposite, left: Floral arrangement for a state banquet.

Opposite, right: *The Norman Gateway and Moat Garden*, by Paul Sandby (1731–1809), *c.*1770

Gardeners have been supplying the castle with vegetables and maintaining its ornamental gardens for many centuries. This eighteenth-century gardener is watering the flowers in the Moat Garden.

Right: *Bridget Holmes*, by John Riley (1646–91), 1686

Bridget Holmes (1591–1691) was a 'necessary woman' employed to clean the royal bedchamber at Windsor Castle. Said to be 96 when her portrait was painted by Riley, Bridget Holmes was well paid for her service. In 1685 her salary was £60, plus £10 10s for her lodgings and £21 5s for 'all kind of necessaries in lieu of Bills'. Her portrait is a rare example of a servant as subject, and may reflect her remarkable age and the fact that she served four kings – Charles I, Charles II, James II and William III – before she died, supposedly aged 100, in 1691.

needs of the sovereign was increasingly delegated to lower-ranking servants.

Until the seventeenth century those servants were exclusively male, apart from the queen's ladies. The Yeomen of the Chamber were responsible for cleaning the privy apartments, while other dirty but essential jobs were also carried out by men. One of the first female servants to be part of the household was Bridget Holmes, the 'necessary woman' who was employed to clean and prepare the royal bedchamber at Windsor Castle. Holmes polished and dusted the furniture and was responsible, with the assistance of other servants, for laying fires, mopping and sweeping, and the unenviable task of emptying and cleaning chamber pots and close stool pans.

Bridget Holmes was only one of the many women and men from the eleventh century to the present day who have worked behind the scenes, largely unnoticed, carrying out the essential tasks without which the castle could not function. Windsor Castle has always had to be cleaned and maintained, its waste disposed of, its people fed, its treasures cared for and its entrances secured. In addition, the castle has required servants for ceremonial purposes, to add to the dignity of the sovereign with a liveried presence, as well as

ensuring that plate glittered, that spectacular meals were served and wine poured and fires kept burning. Over the centuries a whole range of specialist tasks grew up and the royal household expanded into a cumbersome and archaic institution. In the 1840s Prince Albert overcame stiff resistance to reorganise the household under a Master of the Household, a role that still exists today.

The Royal Household has undergone other reorganisations since the nineteenth century and is today a much smaller and more efficient institution than in the past. It is now divided into five main departments. The Private Secretary's Office supports The Queen in her duties as Head of State while the Privy Purse and Treasurer's Office deals with financial and other business matters. The Lord Chamberlain's Office organises those elements of The Queen's programme that involve ceremonial activity, travel and events where The Queen meets the public. The Royal Collection Department is not only responsible for the care and presentation of the Royal Collection but also manages the public opening of the castle. The Master of the Household's Department handles everything involved with official and private entertaining across all the royal residences and therefore includes everyone

Below left: Vacuuming the Garter Throne Room.

Below right: A table is polished to a high shine by 'C' Branch.

Table settings are precisely
measured.

from cooks to French polishers and florists to fendersmiths.

The Master of the Household's Department is divided into different branches. 'F' Branch deal with food, 'H' Branch with housekeeping, 'C' Branch are craftsmen who work closely with the Royal Collection Department, and the General or 'G' Branch encompasses the liveried 'front-of-house' staff who, like many others in the Royal Household, move between Buckingham Palace, Windsor Castle and other residences as required.

The State Apartments are cleaned by a team from 'H' Branch between 7am and 9.30am each day, before the public arrive. Housekeeping Assistants from 'H' Branch are specially trained to clean the works of art on display throughout the castle and to ensure the highest standards of hospitality for Her Majesty's guests, whether that be running a bath or unpacking a suitcase.

For grand banquets and dinners, tables are created from leaves put together by 'C' Branch, who will ensure that any tiny chips and dents are repaired and that the wood is polished to a high shine, while the chairs are lined up using a special stick that measures the exact distance between the back of the chair and the table. Behind the spectacular State Rooms is a warren of passages accessed through hidden doors. They include the Glass, Wax and Silver Pantries, each under the direction of a Yeoman. The Yeoman of the Cellar is in charge of all the wines and spirits served at the castle. Their archaic-sounding titles belie the efficiency and precision with which they and others in the Household must work to ensure that every occasion goes without a hitch.

There are some 300–400 fireplaces in the castle, their fenders kept cleaned and polished by a fendersmith, while the

Horological Conservator (Clockmaker) cares for some 450 clocks in the castle and other buildings. The clocks range from miniatures, barely bigger than a watch, to turret clocks. When the clocks go forwards for British Summer Time, and back again in the autumn, it takes the Clockmaker a whole weekend to correct the time on all the clocks in his care. Each one must be adjusted and corrected for accuracy – except for the clock in the Great Kitchen, which is deliberately kept five minutes fast.

Many of the staff based at Windsor Castle care for the works of art (see Conserving the castle, pp. 86–91), while others are employed to work in the admissions centre or to act as guides or wardens, available to answer questions from visitors. Few of those who come to admire the magnificent rooms will be aware of the work that goes on behind the scenes to ensure that Windsor Castle always looks its best.

THE ROYAL LIBRARY AND PRINT ROOM

The Royal Library is housed in three rooms which were formerly part of the castle's State Apartments. The first room was the Queen's Bedchamber, decorated in the late seventeenth century for Charles II's queen, Catherine of Braganza; the second is within the tower built by Henry VII for his personal use, including the king's private bedroom; and the third, perhaps most famously, was adapted from the Long Gallery built by Elizabeth I as a private space in which she could walk with her ladies when the weather was too bad to go outside.

The Library as it exists today was established by William IV in the 1830s. Earlier Royal Libraries had been presented to the nation: in 1757 by George II and in 1823 by George IV, the collections together forming a core part of today's British Library. However, the books presented by George IV did not include his private collection. He was an avid collector of books, as of much else, with particular interests in military history, classical literature, English literature, history and topography. His father, George III, was also a keen reader as well as a collector, and parts of his extensive collection of books remained in royal ownership after the 1823 gift. These included important early printed books (incunables), and books on agriculture, botany, architecture and science, among other subjects, some of them annotated in his own hand.

When William IV came to the throne in 1830, he brought his brother and father's collections together at Windsor in a new royal

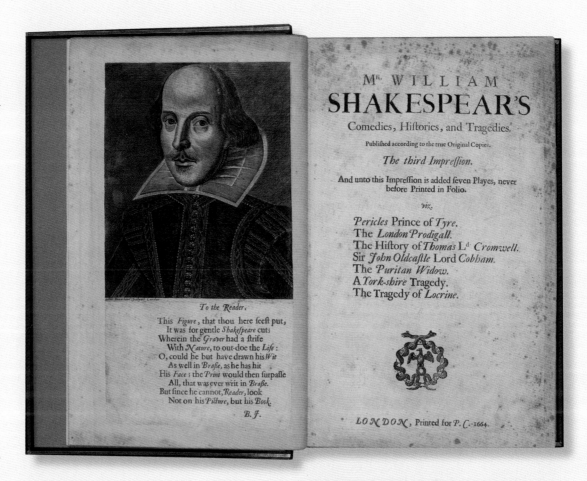

library, and added to it considerably himself. Prince Albert was an energetic organiser and turned his attention to the Royal Library in 1860. With the Librarian, Bernard Woodward, he organised the Library by subject area, an arrangement that remains in place today. The Library continued to be extended during the reign of Queen Victoria, with new books from throughout the British Empire as well as historical material or books with a particular relevance to the monarchy.

The Library's collection has more than quadrupled in size since Prince Albert's reorganisation and now contains more than 200,000 items. It includes all the miniature books written for Queen Mary's Dolls' House and over 500 volumes of works by Shakespeare, with versions of his works in numerous languages, including French,

Right: Mary, Lady Heveningham, by Hans Holbein the Younger (1497/8–1543), *c.1532–43*

Far right: Simon George, by Hans Holbein the Younger (1497/8–1543), *c.1535*

Opposite: The Superficial anatomy of the shoulder and neck, by Leonardo da Vinci (1452–1519), *c.1510–11*

Below: A Greyhound, by Albrecht Dürer (1471–1528), *c.1500–1*

Italian, Portuguese, Georgian and Hebrew.

The Print Room at Windsor Castle is another legacy of Prince Albert's indefatigable energy. Today it houses an outstanding collection of Old Master drawings, including a group of 85 portrait studies by Hans Holbein the Younger and 550 sheets by Leonardo da Vinci, studying figures, anatomy, landscape and much else. Acquired by Charles II, those drawings form the foundation of a collection of drawings that was added to substantially by George III, and now contains important works by Michelangelo and Raphael, as well as Italian baroque drawings; Dutch, Flemish, German and French drawings from the sixteenth and seventeenth centuries; and eighteenth-century Venetian drawings by Canaletto and others. There are large numbers of eighteenth-century English drawings, including many drawings and watercolours of Windsor by Paul and Thomas Sandby. The Print Room is also home to large groups of prints by Dürer, Hollar and others, while thousands of nineteenth-century watercolours relate particularly to Queen Victoria and her family and travels, many of whose own artistic productions are also kept in the Print Room.

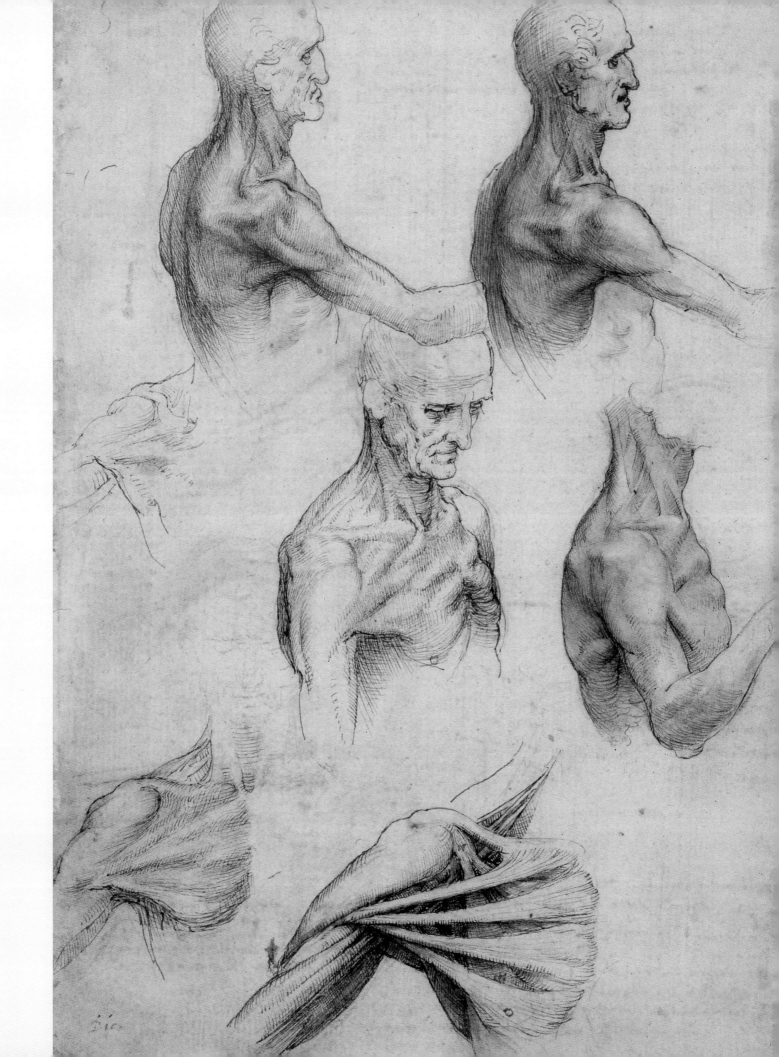

6

THE MODERN CASTLE

Queen Elizabeth II in Coronation Robes, by Sir Herbert James Gunn (1893–1964), 1953–4

The state portrait of Her Majesty The Queen was commissioned to commemorate her coronation, which took place on 2 June 1953. The Queen wears the purple Robe of Estate and a white satin coronation dress decorated with national and Commonwealth emblems, as well as symbols of peace and plenty. Executed in seed pearls, crystals, coloured silks and gold and silver thread, the dress was embroidered by members of the Royal School of Needlework, who worked for a total of 3,500 hours between March and May 1953. The portrait hangs in the Garter Throne Room at Windsor Castle.

Queen Victoria's resistance to change had grown ever more marked as she grew older. Innovation of any kind was strictly forbidden. When curtains or upholstery needed renewal, the article had to be replaced with an exact duplicate. 'On no account may the entire renovation of a room be undertaken all at once', noted one observer. 'It must be done piece by piece in Her Majesty's absence, so that it never loses its look of homeliness.' The walls in the Queen's apartments were densely covered with paintings and photographs, while more photographs with bronze and marble busts and statuettes and other family mementos crowded every other surface.

All this changed with King Edward VII, who reacted against the sombre and cluttered atmosphere. After 'quite a smart difference of opinion' between the King, who wanted to move into his parents' rooms, and Queen Alexandra, who wanted to use the State Apartments, the King had his way and the Private Apartments were made ready for their new occupants. Prince Albert's rooms, which had lain untouched for 40 years, were cleared and his writing room fitted out as a bathroom 'on the latest principle' with white and green cippolino marble. The old Queen's rooms in the Victoria Tower were decorated for

Queen Alexandra, the gloominess lightened with pink satin on the bedroom walls and a bathroom lined with pink and white marble.

The whole of the Upper Ward was modernised, as the King ordered electric light to be extended throughout and had telephones and central heating installed. New bathrooms, lavatories and 'similar apartments' were a priority, which must have been a relief to royal guests. The improvements were noted with approval by Sir Lionel Cust, Surveyor of the King's Pictures, remembering that 'previous visitors to the castle, especially royal visitors, needed to be almost mediaeval in their habits'.

The improvements extended to the State Apartments, where many of the rooms were refreshed and redecorated and much of the accumulated clutter of the past reign cleared out. Over the course of Queen Victoria's reign, the Queen's Guard Chamber and Grand Vestibule had gradually filled with guns, palanquins, horse-trappings and various exotic gifts that had been presented

quite a smart difference of opinion

King Edward VII modernised the Upper Ward, installing electric lighting, telephones, central heating and new plumbing throughout. His own bathroom was fitted out 'on the latest principle' with white and green marble.

to the Queen from all corners of the globe. When inspected, many of the gifts were found to be infested by moth and promptly removed to the Quadrangle, where they were burnt. Other, smaller gifts and tributes were dispersed to other palaces or placed on long-term loan.

While the rooms were being cleared, the

previous visitors to the castle ... needed to be almost mediaeval in their habits

pictures were cleaned and rearranged and on 31 March 1902, the state rooms reopened to the public on what was described as a 'memorable day at Windsor Castle'. 'All day long crowds have been going through the State Apartments', the inspector of the castle wrote to Lionel Cust; 'the Rooms have been full, & from the Entrance a queue has spread its serpentine like form all along the North Terrace to the Office ... there are at least a thousand persons waiting in the Lower Ward ... All those to whom I have spoken are full of praise at seeing the changes.'

Queen Alexandra's sitting room in the Victoria Tower, now known as Queen's Tower, at Windsor.

King Edward VII was famously sociable, and he and Queen Alexandra entertained on a lavish scale. Windsor Castle came to life when he was in residence, usually for the second half of November and the second half of June, with additional visits if required. A garden party for several thousand guests was often given in the East Terrace Garden in late June or July, while the summer visit revolved around the Ascot races, or a chance to enjoy the nine-hole golf course laid out by the King in the Home Park, just below the castle. In November the King and Queen hosted

shooting parties and dinners, and successful West End plays or shows were performed in the Waterloo Chamber. The household required to run the castle to exacting royal standards at these times was a huge one. There was a staff of 60 in the kitchen alone, feeding 200 upper servants in the stewards' room each day, while a further 400 lower servants ate in two sittings in the servants' hall. When the King was in residence, the castle 'hummed like a great city'.

The King's eldest son, Albert Victor, Duke of Clarence and Avondale, had died

he was pernickety about everything being in its right place

of pneumonia in 1892 and his tomb, the masterpiece of the sculptor Sir Alfred Gilbert, now dominates the Albert Memorial Chapel that had been remodelled to the memory of his grandfather, the Prince Consort. His early death meant that on Edward VII's accession, the King's second son, George, became Prince of Wales. King George V, as he became in 1910, was a countryman at heart, and preferred to spend time at Sandringham or Balmoral. Rather like his grandmother, Queen Victoria, he was pernickety about everything being in its right place. Photographs were taken of his desks and tables so that cleaning staff could put everything back exactly after dusting.

King George V might not have been enthusiastic about Windsor Castle but Queen Mary loved the 'dear glorious old castle so full of historical associations'. A great-granddaughter of George III through her mother, Queen Mary was proud of her direct links with the 'old' royal family. She devoted herself to preserving the castle and its collections, which were for her 'a never ending joy', and she spent much effort arranging and rearranging rooms with new acquisitions such as the silver-mounted cocus-wood cabinets, thought to have been made for Queen Henrietta Maria around 1665; they were given to King George V by Lord Rothschild in 1910. The Queen was particularly interested in seeking out items with royal connections and reacquired for the Royal Collection two Brussels tapestries with the arms of William III and Mary II, a pair of giltwood mirrors with the cypher of Queen

Right: King George V, by Sir Oswald Birley (1880–1952), 1934

King George V (1865–1936) wears the 'Windsor Uniform' designed by George III, with the riband, star and garter of the Order of the Garter.

Left: Portrait of Queen Mary, by William Bruce Ellis Ranken (1881–1941), 1923

Queen Mary (1867–1953) loved Windsor Castle and her delight in furniture and in miniature objects can be seen in this portrait of her in the Queen's Sitting Room in the Queen's Tower.

Anne, and Queen Charlotte's jewel cabinet, made in 1762.

Queen Mary's delight in furniture and decoration and in miniature objects led to the creation of the Dolls' House that bears her name and that was presented to her in 1924. Designed by Sir Edwin Lutyens, it was meant to show future generations 'how a King and Queen of England lived in the twentieth century and what authors, artists and craftsmen of note there were during their reign'.

The First World War brought two of Queen Victoria's grandchildren, King George V and Kaiser Wilhelm II, into direct conflict. As head of the House of Saxe-Coburg-Gotha, the King was aware of the widespread feeling that the close ties of the royal family to Germany were awkward when the two countries were involved in such a terrible war. At a Privy Council meeting in July 1917

King George VI at his desk at Windsor Castle during the Second World War, with Princesses Elizabeth and Margaret and Queen Elizabeth.

it was decided to rename the royal family the House of Windsor, a decision that was widely welcomed. 'No better choice could have been made', approved *The Times*. 'It connects the old with the new … Windsor is indeed a loadstar [*sic*] for the descendants of those who have gone forth from these islands and made the new British Empire. Visitors who "come home" from the Dominions want to see Windsor, and make their pilgrimage there.'

As life got back to normal after the war, the public returned to Windsor Castle in such numbers that the Lord Chamberlain had to request extra guides. A suggestion that garden seats be provided on the North Terrace so that visitors could rest their feet was summarily rejected by the Keeper of the Privy Purse on the grounds that the Terrace 'would develop into a temporary restaurant or picnic place with the usual result of litter'.

King George V died at Sandringham on 20 January 1936; his funeral took place in St George's Chapel a week later, the third state funeral to be held at Windsor in a little over 30 years. Shortly afterwards the Royal Librarian, Sir Owen Morshead, walked around the castle with the widowed Queen Mary: 'though she was a thousand miles from any trace of self-pity at any point, it was pathetic to see her looking round over these deserted rooms, which owe everything to her diligence and generosity … and saying "I think we did do a certain amount"'.

During the reign of King George V the Prince of Wales had his own residence, Fort Belvedere, in the Great Park. King Edward VIII, as he became, disliked the 'almost overpowering vastness and formality' of Windsor Castle, whose walls, he said, 'seemed to exude disapproval', and chose to stay at Fort Belvedere after his accession. It was, however, in his rooms at Windsor Castle

The Imperial State Crown with the Black Prince's Ruby, which was removed for safety during the Second World War and buried in a biscuit tin at Windsor Castle.

the most precious of the Crown Jewels were hidden in a biscuit tin and buried deep below the castle

entertaining during Ascot Week.

The Second World War brought many changes. The King remained in London with his immediate staff, but the rest of the Royal Household was evacuated to Windsor Castle and Frogmore. The State Apartments were adapted as offices, and the Queen's Presence Chamber was transformed into a staff recreation room with a billiard table sent over from Royal Lodge. Like everywhere else in the country, blackout blinds and curtains were fitted to every window. External lamps were removed and sent for scrap and roof lights covered over, while basement rooms were made ready for use as shelters if necessary. A shelter for the King and Queen was eventually established on the ground floor of the Queen's Tower, after the roof and external walls had been strengthened with concrete and steel.

Many households underwent preparations for war, but few had to consider the safety of such priceless works of art as were housed at the castle. The Royal Archives were evacuated from the Round Tower to underground spaces within the castle, while the most precious Old Master drawings were sent to the National Library of Wales in Aberystwyth. While some treasures left the castle, others were brought there for safety. On the orders of King George VI, the most precious of the Crown Jewels, including the Black Prince's Ruby from the Imperial State Crown, were removed from the crown, hidden in a biscuit tin and buried deep below the castle. Two secret chambers with steel doors were created under one of the medieval sallyports, and the

that the most significant event of his reign took place on 11 December 1936, when he announced his abdication in a live radio broadcast.

The new King, George VI, and Queen Elizabeth had also had a country residence in the Great Park since 1931: George IV's extensive Royal Lodge, much reduced by William IV, was transformed by them into a comfortable family home. The King and his family continued to reside there, dividing their time between Buckingham Palace and the Great Park, although they used the castle during the Easter season and when

Crown Jewels placed there to prevent them falling into enemy hands.

During the war years Windsor Castle was also home to the young Princesses, Elizabeth and Margaret. The King and Queen stayed in London and travelled to Windsor at weekends, except at the height of the Blitz in autumn 1940 when they returned each evening. The Princesses spent much of their childhood at the castle, where the future Queen was tutored in English constitutional history by the Provost of nearby Eton College. But there was fun to be had, too, with tea parties, dances, film screenings and pantomimes, many of which took place in the Waterloo Chamber. The series of portraits painted by Sir Thomas Lawrence for George IV were taken down for safety, leaving blank walls behind, and a 16-year-old evacuee, Claude Whatham, was invited to decorate the spaces with characters from pantomimes. It was a daunting commission, not least because he had to share a temporary 'studio' in the Grand Reception Room with Sir Gerald Kelly, who was working on the state portraits of the

King and Queen. Kelly, later President of the Royal Academy, had been commissioned to paint the portraits soon after the coronation. The originals were intended to hang in the Crimson Drawing Room, while copies were to be made for official use throughout the Empire. Kelly was still at work on the portraits when war broke out, and he was invited to base himself at Windsor Castle rather than in his London studio. Given a guest bedroom at the castle and dining with the Royal Household, and sometimes with the King and Queen, Kelly appears to have enjoyed his time at Windsor, so much so that there were rumours that he painted the background of the portraits many times over in order to prolong his comfortable stay for the duration of the war.

An artist with a very different style was also at work at Windsor during the war. John Piper was commissioned by Queen Elizabeth to paint a series of watercolours recording the castle for posterity in case of damage in the war. The 26 views of Windsor Castle and the buildings of the Home and

Queen Elizabeth, Queen Consort of King George VI (left), and *King George VI* (right), by Sir Gerald Festus Kelly (1879–1972), 1938–45

Kelly was invited to base himself at Windsor Castle during the war while painting these state portraits.

Great Parks were completed in two series between 1941 and 1944 and are considered to be the most significant commission for the Royal Collection during the twentieth century. Piper portrayed the castle under dark, brooding skies, perhaps reflecting the national mood at the time; King George VI was said to have joked when seeing the completed pictures that the artist seemed to have had very bad luck with the weather.

Happily, Windsor Castle sustained no damage during the war. By the end of August 1945 the court, including the two Princesses, was able to return to Buckingham Palace, while work began on restoring the State Apartments to their pre-war condition. The King revived the Garter ceremonies, which had lapsed since 1911, and the installation of Princess Elizabeth in the Order of the Garter in the Throne Room at Windsor Castle on St George's Day 1948 marked the 600th anniversary of the founding of the Order (see pp. 30–3). The date of the Garter procession was moved from April to June, when better weather was likely and when the Royal Family would in any case be in residence for Ascot.

Princess Elizabeth and The Duke of Edinburgh were married in 1947. It had been intended that they would be given

Windsor Castle, by John Piper, 1941–4

John Piper was commissioned by Queen Elizabeth to paint a series of watercolours recording Windsor Castle for posterity in case of damage during the Second World War. Here the castle and its surrounding buildings evoke a powerful image of imminent threat.

the artist seemed to have had very bad luck with the weather

Sunninghill Park, within the Windsor Crown Estate, as a country home of their own, but the house was badly damaged by fire before they could move in. As events unfolded, it was not until after The Queen's accession in 1952 that the search for a suitable home outside London was resumed. Using Windsor Castle as a base, The Queen and The Duke of Edinburgh considered various options but soon came to the conclusion that the castle itself would serve the purpose just as well, and it has remained their home ever since. Buckingham Palace is a working base in London, but it is at Windsor that they spend many of their private weekends, and its use as a home for more than 60 years has had a profound influence on the atmosphere of the castle.

In the history of Windsor Castle, the twentieth century was notable for the small number of changes made to the castle's fabric. However, maintenance work was continuous and the identification of major structural problems was an essential part of the preservation of the castle. During the winter of 1987–8 a survey found structural movement in the foundations of the Round Tower. Wyatville had doubled the height of the tower for George IV, which had been visually effective, but the additional weight had been bearing down on the unstable chalk rubble of the motte ever since. A concrete ring-beam, supported on piles driven right through the motte into the ground below, had to be inserted in place of the original foundations to stabilise the structure.

A fire at Hampton Court in 1986 prompted another major project at Windsor to improve fire precautions and safety, and to renew mechanical and electrical services throughout the buildings of the Upper Ward. The project, known as Kingsbury, was run by the Property Services Agency, and was planned in three phases, beginning in June 1988. At

The Sitting Room in the Edward III Tower after its redecoration by Sir Hugh Casson, 1959. The redecoration of rooms in the Upper Ward carried out in the late 1950s was intended to be an exemplar of contemporary domestic taste.

the restoration project was a triumph

each phase the rooms affected were to be cleared of their contents, a decision which meant that when fire broke out in the castle in 1992, most of the works of art in the State Apartments were saved.

The 1992 fire had a devastating impact on Windsor Castle, but the restoration project that followed was a triumph, and was not only completed ahead of schedule but under budget. The work was finished in November 1997, just before the fifth anniversary of the fire. On 14 November The Queen and The Duke of Edinburgh held a reception to thank all those who had worked on the restoration project, and a week later, on 20 November, a ball attended by sovereigns of other European countries, members of the Royal Family and 600 other guests marked

the occasion of their Golden Wedding anniversary.

The fire was a traumatic interruption in what had otherwise become, and remains, a well-established pattern of life at Windsor Castle over the course of The Queen's reign. The castle is Her Majesty's country residence throughout the year, except for January, when she is at Sandringham, and August and September, when the Royal Family gathers at Balmoral. For a month at Easter, the full Household or court moves from Buckingham Palace to the castle and The Queen carries out all her official duties in Windsor. These will include a weekly audience with the Prime Minister and audiences or lunches with visiting religious and political leaders. During Easter Court The Queen has continued Queen Victoria's tradition of inviting around 20 guests to 'dine and sleep' at the castle. The guests, usually a mixture of people prominent in public life, are entertained at dinner, after

The Queen holds private audiences with visiting political and religious leaders at Windsor Castle when the court moves there from Buckingham Palace at Easter.

Top: The Queen attends the Royal Windsor Horse Show every year.

Above: Her Majesty receives a trophy from The Duke of Edinburgh after one of her horses wins a race at a Royal Ascot meeting.

Since 2008 an increasing number of investitures have been held in the Waterloo Chamber, and today visiting heads of state on an incoming state visit are as likely to be welcomed at Windsor Castle as in London. These visits are always marked with the pageantry and precision for which the British monarchy is famous.

The Queen keeps her personal horses at Windsor, where the Royal Mews, designed by Wyatville in 1837, was also brought back into regular use soon after her accession. The horses and carriages are based in London but move to Windsor with the rest of the Household for Easter Court, the Garter Day procession and Ascot Week, as well as for state visits. The stables, paddocks and parks mean that the Royal Family is able to enjoy riding, carriage driving, polo and other equestrian pursuits at Windsor. Since the Windsor Improvement Act of 1848 the northern area of the Home Park has been available for public use but the rest remains private, and Windsor Castle continues to be popular with all members of the Royal Family today. It is the setting for many family occasions, from the sombre – the funerals of Queen Elizabeth The Queen Mother and Princess Margaret – to the joyful. The marriage of The Prince of Wales and The Duchess of Cornwall at Windsor was followed by a reception at the castle, while younger members of the Royal Family, including Prince Harry and Princess Eugenie, have chosen to be married in St George's Chapel.

The Great Park is popular with dog walkers and joggers, and events such as the Royal Windsor Horse Show and the Cartier Queen's Cup Final, an important polo tournament, bring others to Windsor, but for most of the public the castle itself remains the main attraction. More than a million visitors pass through its doors every year to

which The Queen leads them to the Royal Library, where a display of specially selected items from the Royal Collection and Royal Archives is laid out.

The castle is full once more for the Royal Windsor Horse Show in May, and for a week in mid-June, which begins with Garter Day and continues with the Royal Family and their guests in residence for the races at Royal Ascot. This is a popular event in the royal calendar, especially when one of Her Majesty's own horses is competing.

Above: The full pageantry of a procession to welcome foreign heads of state is reserved for state visits. Other official visits can be less formal. The former President and First Lady of the United States, Barack Obama and his wife Michelle, were greeted by The Queen and The Duke of Edinburgh after arriving by helicopter for lunch at Windsor Castle in April 2016.

Right: A number of investitures are now held at Windsor Castle.

marvel at the extraordinarily rich and varied collection of paintings and other works of art on display and at the embodiment of a thousand-year history. Windsor Castle today is a thriving community, and welcomes a wider cross-section of people than perhaps at any other time over the past centuries. It is a busy place, a focus of ceremonial and state events, a centre of worship, and a showcase of an outstanding collection of art, to which additions continue to be made. Although much smaller than it once was, the Royal Household runs events with the same meticulous attention to detail and protocol as it has always done. But important as tradition and ceremonial are, Windsor Castle remains a living community, adapting to changing circumstances as it has always done and

finding new ways to make its treasures and
history accessible and engaging for those who
live locally, as well as for visitors from around
the world.

Windsor Castle has stood for more than
900 years, an enduring testament to the power
and prestige of the monarchy. Apart from a
brief period during the Commonwealth, it has
always been a royal castle, but it is a symbol,
too, of continuity and shared traditions that
allow all those who live, work or visit there
a real sense of connection to the past.

Above: Windsor Castle continues to be a family home.
The Queen with five of her great-grandchildren and her two
youngest grandchildren, photographed by Annie Leibovitz
in the Green Drawing Room in April 2016.

Opposite: The wedding of Prince Harry and Meghan Markle,
The Duke and Duchess of Sussex, was held in St George's
Chapel on 19 May 2018.

Overleaf: Windsor Castle has always made a spectacular
setting for the pageantry of the British monarchy. The
Yeomen of the Queen's Body Guard march through the
Quadrangle of Windsor Castle before a state visit.

QUEEN MARY'S DOLLS' HOUSE

The Dolls' House at Windsor was presented to Queen Mary as a symbolic gift from the nation in 1924. Intended as a showcase for British workmanship, it re-creates on a tiny scale of 1:12 every facet of life from the 1920s, and offers a snapshot of contemporary culture. The Dolls' House was made to the highest standards of the time and represents a remarkable feat of collaboration, co-operation and the co-ordination of manufacturers, craftsmen, artists, composers and writers, who together created a miniature house perfect in every detail, with electricity, running hot and cold water, working lifts and flushing lavatories.

The house was the brainchild of Princess Marie-Louise, the youngest daughter of Queen Victoria's daughter Princess Helena.

Marie-Louise was a childhood friend and cousin of King George V, who knew Queen Mary's love of all things decorative and diminutive. The creation of the Dolls' House, designed by the architect Sir Edwin Lutyens, was to be a collaborative venture, the cost and labour divided among as many people as possible, and intended to brighten the difficult days after the First World War. Lutyens held regular 'Dolleluiah Dinners' at the Savoy to persuade contributors to get on board, and with Princess Marie-Louise approached the leading artists, composers and writers of the day. The finished house was the result of a collaboration between 250 craftsmen and manufacturers, 60 artist-decorators, 700 artists, 600 writers and 500 donors. Many of those involved remain

Opposite, left: The Dolls' House, designed by Sir Edwin Lutyens (1869–1944) and presented to Queen Mary in 1924.

Opposite, right: The entrance hall. Some items are so tiny that they can only be picked up with tweezers.

Above: The library is stocked with tiny copies of printed reference books and classics, as well as specially written works by contemporary writers.

champagnes, wines and spirits and beers were donated and chosen by Francis Berry, the senior partner of Berry Bros of St James's Street in London, which remains Britain's oldest wine and spirits merchant. Each tiny bottle was filled using minute glass pipettes, although unfortunately the bubbles had to be removed from the champagne to make this possible.

The Dolls' House has a range of rooms that not only show contemporary products and tastes but also allow a glimpse of royal life. It features a King's Bedroom, its ceiling painted by George Plank, with notes to the first line of the National Anthem subtly interwoven into a garden trellis, and an eighteenth-century-style bed made by the Royal School of Needlework. The royal coat of arms is embroidered in silk at the head of the bed. The bed, like that in the Queen's Bedroom, has a horsehair mattress on top of a box-sprung one, and a hot water bottle placed between the sheets. The house even contains its own set of miniature Crown Jewels: crowns for the King, Queen and Prince of Wales as well as two orbs, a sceptre, the Sword of State and two pairs of spurs. The replica of Queen Mary's crown has a minuscule replica of the famous Koh-i-Noor Diamond. The jewels are in the Strong Room, stored with a silver dinner service for 18 people made by Garrard & Co. Ltd, Crown Jewellers from 1843.

Other rooms are more typical of townhouses of the period. On the top floor are a servant's room and a nursery, complete with jars of boiled sweets, biscuit tins and chocolate boxes with real chocolate inside, as well as exquisitely tiny toys. There is a beautifully decorated saloon, a dining room, a sitting room for the Queen and, perhaps most extraordinary of all, a library stocked not only with tiny copies of printed reference books and the established literary giants, but also with contemporary works, some

household names today. The garage contains cars by Rolls Royce and Vauxhall. On the tiny shelves are tins of Colman's mustard, filled with real mustard, and miniature bottles of champagne by Mumm. There is a Singer sewing machine, threaded and ready for use, and a box of paints by Winsor & Newton.

The house is filled with thousands of objects, painstakingly created by craftsmen around the country. Many of those who contributed were royal warrant holders, and every diminutive detail was re-created – the joints in the furniture are dovetailed, the sheets embroidered with the royal cipher, the chairs properly upholstered and the beds are sprung. The miniature tube contains real Vim, the jars of Tiptree jam by Wilkin & Sons include cherry, strawberry, blackberry, quince and loganberry jam. The gramophone can be fully wound and was supplied with a selection of records, including 'Rule Britannia' and 'God Save the King', but was placed in the Nursery rather than in the main rooms because of the King's antipathy to gramophones: 'G. hates them!' Queen Mary confided.

More than 1,200 bottles of the finest

of them specially written. Princess Marie-Louise contacted 171 renowned authors of the day; only George Bernard Shaw chose not to contribute. However, J.M. Barrie, John Buchan, G.K. Chesterton, Joseph Conrad, John Galsworthy, Robert Graves, Thomas Hardy, Aldous Huxley, Rudyard Kipling, Somerset Maugham, A.A. Milne, Vita Sackville-West and Edith Wharton all donated works, while Sir Arthur Conan Doyle contributed a short story of 500 words in his own handwriting. The house's collection also contains 50 signed and unpublished music scores bound in leather and embossed with the Queen's monogram.

Princess Marie-Louise contacted leading artists in the same way, over 700 of them, to ask them to donate miniature drawings, watercolours, sketches, etchings, lino prints and engravings. Some pieces were for the walls in the house, but others were to be laid flat and stored in two cabinets in the library and drawers in the basement. More than 750 artworks were received, covering a huge range of subjects and styles; those not currently on display in the house are now kept in the Print Room at Windsor Castle.

The Dolls' House was completed in time for the Empire Exhibition held at Wembley in 1924, and was on display for seven months, during which time more than 1.5 million people visited it. The following year it was lent to the Ideal Home Exhibition at Olympia, where an extra charge of a shilling was made to view it, in aid of the Queen's Charitable Fund. Today the Dolls' House is on permanent display at Windsor Castle, and a portion of each visitor's fee is still donated to charity.

THE FIRE OF 1992 AND RESTORATION

On the morning of 20 November 1992, three members of the Royal Collection's staff were in the Private Chapel at Windsor Castle. A modernisation project known as Kingsbury had been running since 1988, with the aim of updating the wiring and heating and installing fire detection and compartmentation systems throughout the Upper Ward. As each phase started, the rooms were emptied of their contents and many of the pictures were stored for convenience in the Private Chapel before being moved to a store in the Home Park. The three of them were discussing the paintings that were due to be wrapped. 'Can you smell burning?', one said after a while, and they joked about lunch being burnt before spotting with horror that the upper part of one of the tall curtains drawn across the altar in the chapel was alight.

It is thought that the fire was ignited by a spotlight behind the right-hand curtain, but at a height that made it impossible for fire extinguishers to reach. The alarm was raised immediately and the emergency services called, but the fire had spread with terrifying speed through the roof voids and was already out of control. In spite of the presence of 200 firefighters from seven brigades, about two hours after the alarm was raised, the commanders of the firefighting operation made the decision to withdraw to defensive boundaries and concentrate all efforts on not letting the fire past those lines. It meant letting large parts of Windsor Castle burn in order to save the rest.

And burn it did, for 15 hours. It devastated a total of 115 rooms and caused £35m of

Above: Windsor Castle on fire, 20 November 1992.

Opposite, left: St George's Hall devastated by the 1992 fire.

Opposite, right: Treasures being removed from rooms that had not yet been affected by the blaze as it raged through Windsor Castle.

damage. Initially the focus was on saving as many works of art as possible. Exceptional works of art were carried out to the Quadrangle to be laid on the grass before being loaded into removal vans and taken to the store in the Home Park and, when that filled up, to the Riding School in the Royal Mews. Meanwhile, a human chain passed priceless books and drawings from the Royal Library and Print Room to safety in the Governor's residence in the Norman Gate. A large painting by Sir William Beechey, *George III and the Prince of Wales Reviewing the Troops*, and a sideboard designed by Pugin located in the State Dining Room had

been boxed in as they were too large to remove for the Kingsbury project and both were completely destroyed. The Beechey was the only painting to be destroyed during the fire.

Inside, Royal Collection staff stood in the doorway of the Grand Reception Room instructing firefighters in breathing apparatus who rescued treasures through the choking black smoke. The incalculably valuable Gobelins tapestries were attached to the walls with Velcro and poppers and came down with a sharp tug. Everything in the room was rescued apart from the recently restored bronze and crystal chandeliers and the 2-ton

The Crimson Drawing Room after the Fire, by Alexander Creswell, 1993

Creswell was commissioned by The Queen to paint a record of devastation of Windsor Castle after the fire. He later painted the rooms after their restoration (see p. 19).

malachite urn, which was simply too heavy to move, although these were ultimately able to be conserved and redisplayed.

The salvage operation was a model of its kind. Almost nothing was broken and nothing went missing, although a pair of Sèvres porcelain busts of Louis XVI and Marie-Antoinette spent the night forgotten under some blankets in the dark corner of a removal van and were returned with apologies the next day. Incredibly, several thousand pieces of glassware used during state banquets survived, in spite of the fact that the Glass Pantry was near the hottest part of the fire. They were discovered the next day in their cabinets, under a ceiling sagging

with the weight of water and debris above. One by one the glasses were handed out and not a single item was broken.

The first of thousands of meetings to discuss the restoration of the castle took place in the Saxon Tower at 9am the next day, while the smoke and steam was still rising from the devastated rooms and firefighters picked their way through the debris, turning over smouldering timbers and hosing down any embers. The atmosphere at the meeting was sombre, but a decision was made on the most urgent priorities, which were to hold up the burnt building and protect it from the rain with a temporary roof.

As the roof was going up, demolition and

Stained-glass window by Joseph Nuttgens (b. 1941) in the new Private Chapel, 1997

After the fire at Windsor Castle in 1992, Prince Philip was closely involved with the restoration as Chairman of the Restoration Committee, and he took a personal interest in the design of the stained-glass windows for the new Private Chapel. In the lower panels, St George in the centre is flanked on the left by a painting of Sir Jeffry Wyatville being rescued from the flames, and on the right by a firefighter. The panels above show Windsor Castle rising from the ashes.

clearance work started and ideas for how to tackle the restoration were soon being debated publicly. There were arguments for leaving the buildings as a ruin and letting wild flowers grow, for a contemporary rebuilding in glass and steel, for putting the rooms back as they had been the day before the fire or for restoring them with absolute authenticity using nineteenth-century techniques. The advantages and disadvantages of various different approaches were considered by an Advisory Committee chaired by The Duke of Edinburgh. It was eventually decided to adopt an approach known as 'equivalent restoration' in those rooms where most of the paintings, furniture and other works of art had survived: the Green Drawing Room, the Crimson Drawing Room, the Grand Reception Room and, after an initial decision to redesign completely, the State Dining Room and the Octagon Dining Room. The final effect would be as the rooms were originally designed, but there would be 'no pedantry behind the scenes'. Modern electrical and mechanical services were installed throughout: dimmer switches for chandeliers, new lifts from the kitchen to the main dining areas, air conditioning, sophisticated fire detection systems. Over the years George IV's original decor had faded, while the curtains and soft furnishings had often been replaced with less lavish versions. The fire gave an opportunity to restore these rooms as far as possible to their condition when they were first made, albeit tempered by modern tastes and modern budgets.

One of the unexpected benefits of the fire was the opportunity to carry out a detailed archaeological survey of the building. In order to deal with damp, the linings of the damaged rooms were removed and the solid walls (of brick or stone) behind

Opposite and left: The largest timber roof built in the twentieth century, the new hammer-beam roof in St George's Hall was designed by architect Giles Dawson and constructed from 350 oak trees using medieval carpentry techniques.

Following page: St George's Hall has been the setting for ceremonial for 700 years. The Queen and The Duke of York are seen here at a presentation of the Guidon to the Royal Lancers in 2017. A guidon is an heraldic banner traditionally carried into battle by cavalry regiments. A rallying point for fighting units, an heraldic banner would have been a familiar device to Edward III, who built the first St George's Hall at Windsor Castle in the fourteenth century.

the oldest substantially unchanged and still working kitchen in the country, and one of the oldest in the world.

The restoration project involved specialists in a wide variety of historical crafts: carpentry, plasterwork, gilding, carving, needlework, upholstery, heraldic painting, and many more. Everything was put back in the best possible condition. Every piece of furniture was reupholstered, cabinets were cleaned, veneers repaired. The carpet in the Green Drawing Room had survived the fire, but its prolonged sousing in the water from the firefighters' hoses had shrunk it slightly. A new border only a few inches wide was woven to fill the gap.

The original programme had envisaged that the restoration would be completed by spring 1998, but in summer 1996 it was decided to aim instead for the symbolic date of 20 November 1997, which would mark the fifth anniversary of the fire and the Golden Wedding of Her Majesty The Queen and The Duke of Edinburgh. It was an ambitious target that put all those involved in the restoration project under a huge amount of pressure, but the deadline was met; the programme was completed six months ahead of schedule and £3 million below budget.

Regilding the interiors absorbed just under half a million leaves of gold.

were exposed, allowing archaeologists and historians to study the castle's development in a way that had not been possible before, and leading to a new understanding of its complex history. A number of extraordinary features were uncovered or reappraised as a result, including a beautifully vaulted medieval corridor in the kitchen area and the original fourteenth-century roof of the Great Kitchen itself, which, it was now realised, was

ACKNOWLEDGEMENTS

Condensing a thousand years of history into a book of this length has been a considerable challenge. I could not have done it without drawing on the work of scholars and experts, most particularly those whose most recent research is presented in *Windsor Castle: A Thousand Years of a Royal Palace*, edited by Steven Brindle and published by the Royal Collection in 2018. I am indebted also to earlier books which have added considerably to my understanding of other aspects of the castle's history. These include Mark Girouard, *Windsor: The Most Romantic Castle* (1993); Annie Gray, *The Greedy Queen* (2017); Adam Nicolson, *Restoration: The Rebuilding of Windsor Castle* (1997); Hugh Roberts, *For the King's Pleasure: The Furnishing and Decoration of George IV's Apartments at Windsor Castle* (2001); Jane Roberts, *Views of Windsor: Watercolours by Thomas and Paul Sandby* (1995); and John Martin Robinson, *Windsor Castle: The Official Illustrated History* (London 2001). I am very grateful, too, to those who have generously shared their knowledge of the castle and taken the time to comment so helpfully on the text, most particularly Kate Owen, Jane Roberts and Richard Williams.

It has been a privilege to learn more about the history of this fascinating building and to work closely with a number of people at the Royal Collection Trust, as well as with designer Briony Hartley. I owe particular thanks to Jacky Colliss Harvey for her encouragement, and to Rosie Bick for sourcing images and dealing so efficiently with the administrative aspects of the project. Finally, I would like to thank project manager Johanna Stephenson for her support and good humour. It has been a pleasure to work with them all.

Malachite urn from the Peterhof Imperial Lapidary Workshop, 1836.

INDEX

First published 2019 by Royal Collection Trust
York House, St James's Palace
London SW1A 1BQ

Reprinted 2022, 2025

ISBN 978 1 909741 64 5
101686

A catalogue record of this book is available from
the British Library

Designer: Briony Hartley
Project Manager: Johanna Stephenson
Project Editor for Royal Collection Trust: Rosie Bick
Production Manager: Sarah Tucker
Colour reproduction: Altaimage London
Printed and bound in Wales by Gomer Press
Printed on Perigord 130 gsm

Title page: The Long Walk, connecting Windsor Castle and the
Great Park. The final section forms part of the processional
route for state visits.

Contents page: The Green Drawing Room, as restored
to its late Georgian appearance after the fire of 1992.

Pages 4–5: Silk and wool Brussels tapestry panel depicting the
coat of arms of William III and Mary II, between the seated
figures of Mars and Minerva.

Pages 34–5: Coat of arms inside the lid of a seventeenth-
century silver-gilt cup, bought by George IV *c.*1826.

Pages 62–3: Large oval serving dish from the richly painted
and gilded 'Harlequin Service', made by Chamberlain & Co.
of Worcester in 1816.

Pages 98–9: A detail from Antonio Verrio's painted ceiling
in the King's Eating Room, now the King's Dining Room,
depicting the Banquet of the Gods.

Pages 132–3: The back of Queen Charlotte's sedan chair,
covered with red morocco leather with elaborate gilded
metal decoration.

Pages 164–5: Axminster carpet in the Green Drawing Room.
Commissioned by Prince Albert, the carpet was entirely
stitched by hand and completed in time to be shown at the
Great Exhibition of 1851.

Front cover: The Crimson Drawing Room, Windsor Castle.

Back cover: The motte and Round Tower, Windsor Castle.

PICTURE CREDITS

All images, unless otherwise stated below, are
© Royal Collection Enterprises Limited 2025 |
Royal Collection Trust.

© His Majesty King Charles III 2025 / Royal Collection
Enterprises Limited p. 130 (below)
Royal Collection Enterprises Limited 2025 / All
Rights Reserved pp. 32 (left), 171, 173, 174, 175, 177;
Photographer: Philip Craven p. 97; Photographer:
David Cripps p. 186 (left); Photographer: Mark Fiennes
front cover, pp. iv–v, vi, 15, 120, 128 (far left), 193;
Photographer: John Freeman pp. 58, 74; Photographer:
Ian Jones pp. 26, 28–9; Photographer: Lisa Linder
pp. 52 (left), 55; Photographer: G. Newbery p. 188;
Photographer: Will Pryce pp. ii–iii, 6, 14, 11, 16–17,
39, 43, 56 (far left), 57, 59, 60, 69, 73, back cover;
Photographer: Peter Smith pp. 70–1, 114–15, 178

Royal Collection Trust would like to thank Bob Marshall
for the creation of images on pp. 8, 10, 23, 25, 37

© The Dean and Canons of Windsor. Photograph:
Royal Collection Trust pp. 18, 31, 41, 49

Royal Collection Trust is also grateful for permission
to reproduce the items listed below:

Alnwick Castle, in the collection of The Duke of
Northumberland pp. 104–5
© 2016 Annie Leibovitz p. 182
Musée de la Tapisserie de Bayeux, France /
With special authorisation of the city of Bayeux /
Bridgeman Images p. 7
© The Trustees of the British Museum p. 93 (right)
Getty p. 191
© New Angle Production Ltd p. 125
© Alamy pp. 26, 27, 33, 92 (right), 123 (both),
124 (right), 179, 180 (both), 181 (both), 183,
190 (right), 196–7
The Burial of Charles I, fresco painting by Charles West
Cope, © Parliamentary Art Collection, WOA 2895;
www.parliament.uk/art p. 50

Every effort has been made to trace and credit all
known copyright or reproduction right holders; the
publishers apologise for any errors or omissions and
welcome these being brought to their attention.